Less is More, Slow is Fast

Building Wealth, Living Healthy, and Increasing American Prosperity in the Knowledge / Innovation Economy

Linkun Shi

Disclaimers:

The goal of the first Part of this book is to provide accurate and useful information to you about personal investment. The book is intended to provide general guidelines that are for informational purposes only and is provided with the understanding that the author is not engaged in rendering professional services or in providing specific investment advice.

The application of general guidelines involving regulatory, accounting, and legal practices, which may differ from locality to locality and which are constantly changing, is highly dependent on an evaluation of individual facts and specific circumstances. With regard to any decisions that can potentially have significant financial, legal, tax, or other consequences, no book can take the place of individual professional advice. You should not regard this book as a substitute for consulting with a competent lawyer, accountant, or other financial professional, as appropriate to the nature of your particular situation.

The book presents various investment strategies and products that may or may not be appropriate for your specific situation. It is also important to keep in mind that different types of investments involve varying degrees of risk, and there can be no assurance that the future performance of any specific investment, investment strategy, or product discussed in this book will be profitable or suitable for your portfolio. Also, in order to help you consider investment options, this book makes certain assumptions about future investment returns. These projections are based on a number of factors, including past performance of various asset classes. While the past sometimes repeats itself, there is no assurance that past investment performance will be indicative of future results. Consequently, future investment performance for asset classes and portfolios cannot be guaranteed. If you have any questions regarding the applicability of any investment strategy or products discussed in this book to your particular financial situation, you should consult with a professional advisor.

References in the book to products, service providers, and potential sources of additional information do not mean that I can promise for such products or services or the information or recommendations in those sources. I am not responsible for any third-party product or service or content over which I do not have control.

Part Two of his book is not intended as a substitute for the medical advice. This book is not intended as a substitute for the medical advice of physicians. The reader should regularly consult a physician in matters relating to his/her health and particularly with respect to any symptoms that may require diagnosis or medical attention.

This book was prepared or accomplished by Linkun Shi in his personal capacity. The opinions expressed in this article are the author's own and do not reflect the view of the Office of Hospital Facilities, the Department of Housing and Urban Development, or the United States government.

Copyright © 2013 by Linkun Shi

All rights reserved. No part of this publication may be reproduced, distributed, or transmitted in any form or by any means, including photocopying, recording, or other electronic or mechanical methods, without the prior written permission of the publisher, except in the case of brief quotations embodied in critical reviews and certain other noncommercial uses permitted by copyright law.

Praise for the book:

"Very interesting and thought provoking information" -- Zachary K. Kau, Director, Healthcare Finance, Bank of America Merrill Lynch

Table of Contents

PREFACE 7

AN OVERVIEW 17

PART ONE - INVESTMENT 21

CHAPTER 1 BET ON THE JOCKEYS 21
CHAPTER 2 WONDERFUL COMPANIES 24
CHAPTER 3 FAIR PRICES 29
CHAPTER 4 EMOTIONAL INTELLIGENCE, MIRROR NEURONS, AND CONTRARIAN INVESTORS 31
CHAPTER 5 THE FORMULA 37
CHAPTER 6 PATIENCE AND LONG TERM PROSPECTIVE 82

PART TWO - HEALTH 84

CHAPTER 7 AN ANCIENT SECRET RECIPE ON DIETING 84
CHAPTER 8 FOOD NUTRITION 90
CHAPTER 9 ECZEMA, ASTHMA, SLEEPING DISORDERS, AND JOINT PAINS 100
CHAPTER 10 AGING IS MERELY A CURABLE DISEASE 105

PART THREE - GOVERNMENT, HEALTH CARE, HOUSING, STEM, AND KNOWLEDGE ECONOMY 109

CHAPTER 11 GOVERNMENT: THE PARTY – WHICH PARTY? 109
CHAPTER 12 JOBS: CHINA, INC. AND U.S.A., INC. 127
CHAPTER 13 HOME OWNERSHIPS AND HEALTH CARE 144
CHAPTER 14 STEM FIELDS, HIGH-TECHS AND ENTREPRENEURSHIPS 155
CHAPTER 15 KNOWLEDGE / INNOVATION ECONOMY, TALENTS, EDUCATION AND TEACHER PAYS 161

GLOSSARY 164

ABOUT THE AUTHOR 183

INDEX 184

PREFACE

"Po: Maybe I should just quit and go back to making noodles.

Oogway: Quit, don't quit? Noodles, don't noodles? You are too concerned about what was and what will be. There is a saying: yesterday is history, tomorrow is a mystery, but today is a gift. That is why it is called the 'present'."-- Kung Fu Panda

I was born at the beginning of Cultural Revolution in scenic, yet backward Kunming City, Yunnan Province, China. During the Cultural Revolution, Mao Tse-tung closed all universities and colleges in China, and discouraged knowledge learning and studies. I didn't do any real studies until late of my sophomore year in high school when my little girlfriend stopped talking to me because her parents wanted her to stay focus on studying for her exams to getting into a good high school in Kunming City. Only after Deng Xiaoping took power and started reforms and restored college entrance exams in 1978, gradually students were encouraged to learn again. My college entrance exam was one year away, and my girlfriend high school entrance exam was two years away. College Entrance Exam scores have been the main criteria to get into colleges in China, GPAs are usually not considered. My girlfriend was three years younger than me. I was upset after she stopped talking to me, and but channeled my anger to studies.

With Deng's reform, China added a third year to high school, so luckily I got one extra year to turnaround myself. My hormone cooled down a bit by not around my girlfriend. I started thinking about where life was going for the first time and decided to study hard for the entrance exam. I determined to excel on my college entrance exam to prove she made a "mistake". I studied 17 hours a day every day or about 119 hours a week for two years. Until then I had never studied or worked so hard in my whole life.

I was studying most of the times except sleeps, meals; brief exercises and commutes to and from school. Fortunately also the same year, our school assigned us a great English teacher - Ms. Yu. Not only she knew English well, at that time was rare, especially in Kunming, but she also cared about whether we learned. Her teaching method was different, but effective. Our prior English teacher was a no-good, time wasting bad teacher who taught himself English. I often failed his English exams or quizzes. He enjoyed announcing my quiz or exam grades, usually the last few students, and handed me the grades in front of the whole class. It was humiliating.

With Ms. Yu as my teacher, my English improved quickly. Within a year, I ranked top in our English class. With the improved confidence, my grades in other subjects also got better. Ms. Yu turned my life around. Two years ago, my teacher had told my parents that I had slim chance to getting into any college. My teacher ranked me at the bottom few in a class of 60 students. My high school Kunming Number One High School was one of the top two high schools in the city.

I got accepted at Sun Yat-sen University (Zhongshan University), a top ten college in China to study botany. Most colleges had few major choices. Colleges further reduced choices of majors for students coming from less developed provinces such as Yunnan Province. In 1984, I went to Sun Yat-sen University. That year, out of the 1.64 million high school graduates in China took the College Entrance Exams, 480 thousands got accepted, or 29.3 percent got accepted. At that time, government provided tuition free educations, and even free room and board. After college, I came to the US to pursue a graduate study in Biology. After receiving my master's degree, I did molecular immunology research at Harvard Medical School. While at Harvard Medical School, we publish a research paper: The 4F9 Antigen Is a Member of the Tetra Spans Transmembrane Protein Family and Functions as an Accessory Molecule in T Cell Activation and Adhesion (Nojima, et al., 1993).

After working briefly at two large pharmaceutical companies, I went to Business School for a MBA upon receiving a full tuition scholarship for two years.

During the Cultural Revolution, China banned all private business enterprises. My civil engineer parents had combined salaries above average at 60 RMB (about $8) a month. In 1978, after meeting with Lee Kuan Yew - Prime Minister of Singapore, Deng Xiaoping started economic reforms at four Special Economic Zones – Shengzhen, Zhuhai, and Shantou in Guangdong Province near Hong Kong, and Xiamen in Fujian Province near Taiwan. When I started junior high school in 1978, my granduncle Weijing Hu introduced me to stamp collections. My maternal grandfather died when my mother was 3 after Japan invaded China. My granduncle adopted my mother when my mother was in junior high school because my grandmother could barely support two children.

My granduncle Hu was a physics professor at Yunnan University. He had no children and never been married. He liked collecting stamps and books. He became the Vice Chairman of Yunnan Philatelic Society and one of the original Board Member of China National Philatelic Association. The stamps I collected helped me paid the airline tickets to the U.S. Collecting Stamps was my first investment. A new 8 cents RMB (about 1 penny US) 1980 Chinese monkey stamp is now worth US$2,000, which equals to a 200,000% return. A few Chinese Cultural Revolution stamps released in the late 1960s appreciated even more. Some Chinese stamps fetch more than one million dollars (Chow, 2013). Good long-term investments can have big payoff.

I met Warren Buffett for the first time in 1996 in New York, during my second year in business school. I worked for Dr. Robert Mockler, a management professor. He and his late brother Coleman Mockler, CEO of Gillette Company, and Mr. Buffett knew each other. Dr. Mockler invited Mr. Buffett to give a talk to our Business School students and faculties. Dr. Mockler asked me to greet Mr. Buffett and bring him to meet our university president.

Mr. Buffett came by himself in a stretch limo. He wore a grey long wool coat probably bought in 1980s, carrying a briefcase full of paperwork. As a billionaire, he had no bodyguards or assistants to carry his stuff. I told Mr. Buffett that I was Dr. Mockler's graduate assistant. He did not hear clearly, so he said, "come again". I repeated that I was Dr. Mockler's graduate assistant. While we were talking, I failed to notice that the elevator doors closed on Mr. Buffett. Later that evening when his limo came to pick him up to the airport, I asked him whether I could take a picture with him. He did not say yes. Mr. Buffett was famous for that he was good at say no to people. Years later, I saw my wife's girlfriend posted her picture on Facebook. She took a picture with Mr. Buffett in a parking lot in Omaha. I am still wondering whether Mr. Buffett refused for picture because of the elevator doors or because I was not an attractive girl.

Before Mr. Buffett's arrival, Dr. Mockler arranged his trip. Mr. Buffett wanted to know details with the talk and travel arrangement, and Mr. Buffett wanted no surprises. Mr. Buffett had a limo to take him to his private jet after the talk. Dr. Mockler asked whether I wanted to take a limo ride with Mr. Buffett, him, and Dr. Mockler's wife. The ride would take less than one hour and driver would drop me to my home around 1 AM. My girlfriend at that time said she didn't want me to come home that late, plus I happened to have an accounting exam the next morning. So I said no to the once in lifetime limo trip with Mr. Buffett. What was I thinking?! Years later, a lunch date on eBay with Mr. Buffett cost more than $2 million.

Before Buffett's seminar, I watched a couple recorded videotapes that Buffett gave talks in other colleges. I read "The Warren Buffett's Way" book by Robert Hagstrom. At that time, there were limited books analyzing Warren Buffett's methods. Mr. Buffett's investment methods appeared to be so simple that people had hard time believing the approaches. After my MBA, I worked for a couple accounting firms as a financial auditor. In the late 1990s, Internet bubbles grew larger. The media claimed that Mr. Buffett's investment method no longer worked in this new age. The stock prices of Yahoo!, Amazon.com, and Qualcomm jumped higher. Many Internet stocks had little revenues, no profits, but huge market capitalizations. The Internet mania spread. Many investors abandoned fundamental stock selection criteria, such as profitability, favoring easy and quick money in the Internet stocks.

While as an audit associate at BDO Seidman, LLP, I audited hedge funds with various trading and investment strategies. My biggest client was Renaissance Technology, Inc. James Simons started the hedge funds trading commodities with a government grant. He had grown the fund to $3 billion under management. He traded everything from stock equities, bonds, foreign currencies, commodities, to complex swaps.

As Warren Buffett stated, "Investing is not a game where the guy with the 160 IQ beats the guy with the 130 IQ". What needed is control of your emotions. I had no knowledge or interest in EQ (Emotional Intelligence Quotient), until my wife and I had issues involving my in-laws. One of the counselors introduced me the importance of EQ after a couple of counseling sessions. I will discuss a few methods I learned to improve emotional intelligence. People can be more productive and have a happier life with higher EQ. EQ, unlike IQ, can be learned and raised (Goleman, Emotional Intelligence: Why It Can Matter More Than IQ , 2005) (Bradberry & Greaves, 2009).

Being a contrarian, going against the crowd, is hard, such as during the Internet bubbles of late 1990s and during the housing bubbles before 2007. Even you might have thought that the bubbles won't last forever, but it was difficult to stay away or even go against the crowd. Recent neuron science findings of mirror neurons indicated that our human brains are wired to share other people's feelings (NOVA, 2005). In a way, the human emotions are connected through a large web. By observing, the mirror neurons help us to experience what the other human are experiencing. The evolution of mirror neurons helped human to learn knowledge actively and making tools in minutes or hours. Passive evolution took generations in animals without mirror neurons. Because of mirror neurons, people have difficulty to disconnect from others' feelings. That is reason for herd mentality in investing.

Over the years, I have studied various successful investors. I will discuss the most important aspects of successful investing and how to analyze them and why they are important, and when to sell your stocks. I will discuss an investment formula that will build your wealth.

I have organized the book into three parts: Part One discusses investments. Part Two discusses healthy living. Part Three discusses macro environments: governments, jobs, health care, housing and education. Each part is self-containing, so you can read the parts in any order you prefer.

Part Two discusses healthy living. We wish for longevity and healthy bodies. We not only want to live longer, but also live healthy while aging. Before starting my MBA program, I joined a large direct marketing health care product company. I attended a few company-sponsored presentations on vitamins. I learned the important role that vitamin C plays in heart and cardio vascular system. A doctor at one presentation indicated the possibility to eradicate cardiovascular diseases with vitamin C.

The diets I have now are different from what I used to eat in China. My parents sent me to live with my uncle's family in a rural village in Henan Province when I was four for two years. Like most rural peasants then, my uncle's family ate meat only once a year during the Chinese New Year festival. We did eat a lot fresh vegetables and fruits right from our own fields and yard. The hygiene conditions were primitive. Our windows were made of paper. There was no tap water, no electricity, no highways, or hospitals around. My uncle's family and I were all relatively healthy, even during wintertime when the temperature could be 2 degree Fahrenheit below zero. "The China Study: The Most Comprehensive Study of Nutrition Ever Conducted And the Startling Implications for Diet, Weight Loss, And Long-term Health" indicates that almost all modern diseases, such as cancers, heart diseases, diabetes, and strokes are caused by eating too much food, especially animal origin proteins and eating processed foods (Campbell & Campbell II, 2006).

Over the past decades, scientists have been trying to find ways to extend life spans. Scientists added ingredients to foods of or injected of various substances to the lab animals, but almost none worked. They did discover that calorie restriction increased the life spans of the animals. With reduction of the mice's food intakes by half, the lab mice' life spans increased 100% comparing with control group. Also the mice with reduced calories looked younger and had more vigor (Walford & Weindruch, 1988). Then scientists also confirmed same findings of calorie restriction with other animals ranging from flies, bugs, monkeys, and other animals. Because the human life span is much longer, the human experiments are still ongoing. By analyzing centenarians, scientists have observed generally low calories in their diets. Even people understand that we need to eat less, but staying with a diet program is the problem.

When I grew up, I was generally skinny and under-weighted. One major reason was that before I went to college, the Chinese government rationed both rice and meat because of the centrally planning government policies. Before I went to high school, our family ate meat once or twice a week. My BMI (body mass index) was nearly too low to disqualify me for college. Sun Yat-sen (Zhongshan) University is located in Guangdong Province. Guangdong was the richest province in the 1980s. I could eat meat every day, or even eat meat three times a day - breakfast, lunch, and dinner. I gained 30 pounds to 120 pounds in one year.

After college I more or less maintained that weight until I graduated from business school and started working as a financial auditor. During audits of manufactures, we dined and ate huge dinners with wines, and then more desserts every night. My co-workers were happy because clients paid for the meals. After a few months, I gained 50 pounds to more than 180 pounds. I had to keep buying new pants and underwear every couple months because the old ones wouldn't fit anymore. At that speed, I would be approaching 300 pounds within a year. I changed to a different accounting firm without manufacture clients. My weight dropped 20 pounds. Dieting is hard. Another reason is that the media had so much conflicting information on losing weight. The commercials always have magic pills, wonderful exercise programs, and lean meals to sell to you for losing weights. I tried a couple of the products, none of those worked. I tried to exercise more, but I ended up eating more after workouts, no weight loss.

Weight-losing formula is simple: if calorie intake is less than calorie use, you will lose weight. The question is how to achieve consistency.

I have a blog in Chinese on 163.com. A blog friend posted a great article on dieting. After doing research on the topic, I knew this diet method is the one I would use, and it would work. I followed this simple method for over three months, and I lost 30 pounds. My weight dropped from 158 to 128 pounds. At first, my wife said I would not able to follow it through and I would get sick if I followed it. I followed the simple and easy method and lost 30 pounds without much exercises. At the end my health improved too, because I restricted my calorie intakes.

During the summer of 2012, my family took a trip to Disney World in Florida. Because I was using my frequent flyer mileages, my wife and kids were taking different airlines. On my way back to New York City, at the Orlando Airport checkpoint, the airport security stopped me and asked me to take my belt out and raise my hand. I was wearing my old jean. After I lost 30 pounds, my jean cannot stay in place by itself without a belt. I told the security guard that I couldn't raise both hands without a belt, but he did not care my appeal. I didn't realize until then losing weight had such side effect. I stroke a difficult pose with both hands raised. I passed the checkpoint. Once inside the terminal, I called my wife and told her this episode.

One important part of healthy living is emotional health, or emotional intelligence (EQ). People smoke, drink alcohol, and even use drugs to relieve emotional distress, which arises from big arguments, quarrels, and fights with someone. The emotional toll can be large if the problems are with someone close. If one experiences ongoing mental stress, he or she can become mentally and physically ill.

I will also discuss supplements to help some health issues. For example, I used to have insomnia problems. I took over-the-counter sleep medicines, prescription Ambien, Ambien CR, drink beers or wines at night just to fall asleep. The problems with these medicines are the side effects and headaches the next days, and habit forming. One day, I found melatonin – the natural brain substance controlling sleep cycles. It was helpful to my sleep. I will discuss my children's eczema and asthma problems and methods we used to cope with their conditions.

Last part of this book discusses what USA can learn from the fast growing countries - China, Singapore and South Korea. With the federal government shutdown for 16 days in October 2013, many problems surfaced. The deep problems are both political and economic. In the past 30 years, China, Singapore and South Korea had an average 10.50 percent, 7.56 percent, and 7.55 percent GDP growth per year respectively (IMF Report for Selected Countries and Subjects, 2013).

With the rapid economic growth, China raised 500 million people out of extreme poverty. China became the second largest economy in the world (Morrison, 2013). Singapore has become a developed country with one of the highest GDP per capita and high life expectancy. Singapore has surplus in both central governmental pension plans and governmental health care accounts for its citizens. South Korea's conglomerates have grown rapidly. Samsung Electronics has become the number one company in information technology and heavy industries. Singapore, South Korea, and Shanghai City of China now have the best public school systems in the world.

USA's GDP growth in the last 30 years has been growing at 3.4 percent per year (IMF Report for Selected Countries and Subjects, 2013). Although, we can argue that USA's GDP per capita has been high. GDP per capita of fourteen countries are higher than the US. Five countries' GDP per capita are twice or more of the US' number (CIA The World Factbook, 2013). Recent governmental shutdown shows many structural and political problems. In 2012, Forbes magazine published an article "Think Social Security's Trust Fund Is a Scam? Medicare Has One Too" (Matthews, 2012). According to governmental data, our Medicare Fund will run out of money in 2024, and social security fund will deplete its Fund in 2033 (SSA, 2013). I will discuss major causes and my suggestions to fix these problems based on the studies of countries that did well in those areas.

Looking ahead into the future, my wife and I sometimes discuss what the good careers will be when our children grow up. I am interested in what the good future jobs will be and world economy will become. By studying a few well-positioned countries and companies, I will discuss the future economy, jobs and how USA and ordinary people can best positioning for the 21st century.

"At today's rate of change, we will achieve an amount of progress equivalent to that of the whole 20th century in 14 years."
-- Ray Kurzweil

An Overview

"We select our marketable equity securities in much the same way we would evaluate a business for acquisition in its entirety. We want the business to be (1) one that we can understand, (2) with favorable long-term prospects, (3) operated by honest and competent people, and (4) available at a very attractive price." -- Warren Buffett 1977

The most important thing in investing is not super high return, because a high return usually comes with a high risk. The most important thing is not losing money. If you don't lose money, with a decent annual return, you will accumulate fair sum of money because the law of compounding interest. As Warren Buffett said "Rule Number 1: Never lose money. Rule Number 2: Never forget rule Number 1". The key elements of investing are betting on great people, investing in companies that have competitive advantages, buying great companies at fair prices and maybe cheap prices, and investing for the long run.

The safest investments are US government treasury bonds comparing to other available investment choices. US government bonds are safe due government's power to tax. So far US government has never defaulted on its Treasury bond or note obligations yet. The Treasury bond returns are fixed. Next best choices are major stock index Electronic Traded Funds (ETF) and major index mutual funds. For example S&P 500 index includes 500 largest and strongest companies. Individual stock picking can be interesting but usually requires more works and often has more risk. You can reap huge rewards by picking the right stocks over the long run.

The problems with investments are that the world is changing at accelerating speed; companies and investors are evolving too. We need a formula that is both flexible yet its key elements stay relatively stable. We want to somewhat automate our investment process. I will go over key components in details of my investment formula in chapters 1 to 5. You can use this investment formula for your stock selections. You can also add or modify elements for your preferred investment selections. After you make a good investment, you don't need to do much for a while. So you can take your time before investing, using a formula or a checklist.

Chapter 1 discusses the method of filtering and ranking key people of companies.

Chapter 2 discusses the method of picking a company with good returns and competitive advantages.

Chapter 3 discusses the method of ranking fair priced or cheap stocks.

Chapter 4 discusses not to follow the herd mentality: EQ, mirror neurons and contrarian investing. This chapter talks about why emotional health is important to your physical health and ways to improve your EQ.

Chapter 5 discusses how to put the formula together.

Chapter 6 discusses how to stay investing for the long term. It is a life style choice.

Part Two of this book is on healthy living. Anyone who has tried different dieting methods knows how hard is to stick to a dieting program. Losing weight appears to be an easy math: you lose weight if the calorie intake is less than your calorie usage. You will lose weights by either reducing calories intakes or by burning more calories.

Chapter 7 discusses a simple ancient Chinese method of losing weight without involving any exercises or spending much money. This method will do much good to your monthly budget that you can spend more money on health supplements that I will mention in chapter 7. A family doctor told me that "invest in your children's education and invest in adults' health".

Chapter 8 discusses the nutrition and important roles vitamin C plays in eradicating or reducing heart diseases and cardiovascular diseases. I will discuss essential supplements for maintaining good health.

Chapter 9 discusses a few ailments and remedies, such as insomnia, skin problems, eczema, and asthma.

Chapter 10 discusses new development in aging, stem cells, and the future of the biotechnology and medicine.

If you want to read health related chapters first, you can jump to chapter 6.

Part Three is on governments, health care, housing, jobs loss and job creation, and education in this knowledge economy (Knowledge economy, 2013).

Chapter 11 discusses the economic development of China over the last 40 years and what USA can learn from the rapid developments in China and Singapore.

Chapter 12 discusses how China, Singapore, and South Korea created millions of jobs and transformed their countries. USA can learn valuable lessons from these countries in creating jobs, increasing competitiveness, and turning budget deficits around in this new world.

Chapter 13. Singapore's home ownership is 90 percent. The percentage is higher than the 70 percent in the USA. Singaporeans' life expectancy is also higher than the USA, while its healthcare expense is 4.6 percent of its GDP and its governmental health care account has a surplus. USA's health care expense is 17.9 percent of GDP with lower life expectancy and our Medicare Fund will run out of money in 2024. In 2013, Bloomberg ranked Hong Kong and Singapore the 1st and 2nd places of the World Most Efficient Health Care. USA was ranked 46th

(Bloomberg, 2013). I will discuss the causes and suggest solutions for the problems.

Chapter 14 focuses on resources and talents on Science, Technology, Engineering, and Mathematics (STEM). USA can grow jobs and gain GDP growth. Small entrepreneurships are hard to achieve critical mass and compete in modern global economy. I will suggest ways for the USA startups to compete.

Chapter 15. World economy has moved into knowledge / innovation economy age. To succeed in this economy, USA needs to improve primary and secondary public education, attract and keep talents, and recruit top third graduates into teaching profession.

"To secure ourselves against defeat lies in our own hands, but the opportunity of defeating the enemy is provided by the enemy himself." Sun Tzu's The Art of War

PART ONE - Investment

Chapter 1   Bet on the Jockeys

"I pick the jockeys, and the jockeys pick the horses and ride them. You guys are the ones I'm betting on, so you figure it out." – When Ross Perot gave Steve Jobs $20 million

This investment formula requires multiple step ranking processes. People factor is usually hard to quantify, or to apply to a formula. Warren Buffett said he wanted to invest in a company with honest and competent management.

I have been pondering on how to rank key people. One day, I noticed Time magazine ranks 100 most influential people in the world annually. Harvard Business Review has an annual list of 100 Best Performing CEOs in the World, and Forbes has a 40 under 40 List.

If you can invest the best, why go the second tier people or the third tier ones. Bloomberg recently reported that Buffett's Berkshire Hathaway just minted another billionaire – Stewart Horejsi (Teitelbaum, 2013). Horejsi bought 40 shares of Berkshire Hathaway shares for $265 each in 1980. And he purchased more. Now he owns 5,800 Berkshire A shares even after selling 1,000 shares in 1998. In September 2013, the Berkshire A share was worth $170,000 each. If you have hundreds of Berkshire shares, you are a millionaire; and if you own thousands of Berkshire shares, you are a billionaire. Besides Buffett, at least 6 current or former billionaires have derived their fortune from Berkshire. They include Charles Munger, the company's vice chairman and David Gotteman, founder of asset management firm First Manhattan Co. All bet their fortune on Warren Buffett.

Company stocks are securities. Security is a form of investment contract. Supreme Court of the United States defined what belongs to investment contracts in the case of Securities and

Exchange Commission vs. W. J. Howey Co., 328 U.S. 293 (1946). To determine whether an instrument qualifies as a security, it must: 1) investment of money due to 2) an expectation of profits arising from 3) a common enterprise, 4) which depends solely on the efforts of a promoter or third party (Russ, 2010).

We invest in stocks with an expectation of profit. The profit depends solely on the efforts of people of the company.

The Harvard Business Review 100 Best-Performing CEOs in the World ranked the total shareholder return since first day of job. They based the review on over 3,000 public traded companies in the world. The number one ranked on the list in 2013 is Steve Jobs of Apple. From 1997 to 2011, Jobs increased Apple's market capitalization by $359 billion, or a 6,682% total shareholder return. Number 2 ranked Jeffrey Bezos of Amazon.com increased its company capitalization by $111 billion, a 12,431% total shareholder return from 1996 to 2013 (100 Best-Performing CEOs in the World, 2013).

Time ranks the World's 100 Most Influential People every year. Time ranked Elon Musk number 2 under titans. After the publication of Time 100 in April 2013, Musk's Tesla Motors stock price quadrupled from $40 to over $190 over the next few months. Musk is a serial entrepreneur who founded Paypal, SolarCity, and SpaceX.

When billionaire Ross Perot invested money with Steve Jobs after Steve left Apple, Perot said I invested in jockey and the jockey picked the horse a ride.

You don't need to pick many companies to invest in. What you need to do is picking one or a few good ones, and holding on to the stocks.

"One genius can feed millions of others. For the upcoming era where creativity will be the most important driver of business success, we need to hire the best. The economic value of one genius is more than $1 billion." -- Lee Kun-hee, Chairman of Samsung Electronics

Chapter 2   Wonderful Companies

"It's far better to buy a wonderful company at a fair price than a fair company at a wonderful price. -- Warren Buffett

"We just focus on a few outstanding companies."-- Warren Buffett

Besides world-class people running a company, what are characters of a wonderful company? A wonderful company must have track record of profitability and good shareholder returns over the years. How do we treat hi-tech companies that have no profitable year or quarter yet? For these hi-tech companies, founders must have profitable track record and great returns to shareholders. Otherwise, a company may have similar fates of many Internet companies in 2000. You may never see a profit ever.

When you have extra money, the safest way is to put into a saving account or buy a certificate of deposit (CD) from banks, maybe at 1% annual interest rate. Banks turn around and lend your money to individual or commercial borrower at higher interest rates. Banks can lend money to credit worthy individuals for a 30-year mortgage at 5% annual rate. Thus, banks make the 4% difference in interest rate. Banks can lend money to less credit worth homebuyers or more risky businesses, say 10%. These kinds of mortgages are known as subprime loans. Then banks can make 9%. What happens if the borrowers fail to pay back loans? If only a small part of borrowers fail to pay back, banks can still weather it. If a larger part of borrowers fails to pay back, banks can go bankrupt.

Because Federal Deposit Insurance Corporation (FDIC) insured up to $250,000 per account, per insured bank, your money are generally safe up to that limit. The banks may go under, unless the federal government bails the banks out. The federal government bailed out many banks in 2008.

By deposit money in banks to earn interest income, you still need to combat the inflations. If the annual inflation rate is 3%, and a bank pays 2% for a one CD, you are losing buying power. One good way to combat inflation is to buy Treasury Inflation-Protected Securities (TIPS).

Another way to combat inflation is buy top rated, or investment grade corporate bonds. Moody's and Standard & Poor, and Fitch rate corporate bonds based on the bonds' credit worthiness. Higher credit company bonds pay lower interest rates than bonds with lower credit ones. Non-investment grade bonds are called high yield bonds, or junk bonds. High yield bonds have higher risks of defaulting.

When a company defaults its bond obligations and files for bankruptcy, any non-liquid assets are sold to pay for debt claims. If a company has more assets than its liabilities, then the company has a positive equity, or positive retained earnings. An individual's or a family's equity is like a company's equity or retained earnings. With a positive equity, at bankruptcy the company often can sell assets to satisfy all outstanding debts. Debts are paid in the order of priority claims. Here are the priorities of claims:

Unpaid salaries and government taxes have the highest priority.

Secured or collateralized bonds or loans

Debentures or general companies bonds

Preferred stocks

Common stocks

If a company has large negative equity, mostly likely the common stock holders will lose everything. Corporate bondholders will lose part of or all principals.

Five-Year Average Revenue Growth Rate

We have heard or read Warren Buffett's statement of investing in companies with sustainable competitive advantages and high return on invested capital. Warren Buffett considered the profitability history of a company more important than a great performance in one year. If a company can achieve high sales growth and return on capital over 5 years, this company usually has certain sustainable competitive advantages. You can find the 5-year sales growth data in many financial services sites, such as MSN money.

When company's sales grow year after year, the company can be in a rapid expanding industry or sector, or the company is eating many other companies' lunches. For example, Samsung's successes come from spotting areas that are small but growing fast. You might ask that why I don't use five-year average net profit growth rate instead. First, my formula will use return on capital, which I will talk shortly. Return on capital measures profitability. Second, companies in slow growing industries can achieve better net profit margin through cost cutting over a few year period, while sales stagnate or is declining.

Return on Capital (ROC)

Return on capital (ROC) is like the ratio return on equity, but different. You can find the return on capital data from many financial service companies. If you are interested, here is the formula to calculate the return on capital (Return on Capital, 2013).

ROC = (Net Operating Profit - Adjusted Taxes) / (Book Value of Debt + Book Value of Equity – Cash)

Company's equity equals total assets minus total liabilities. When total assets are more than total liabilities, a company has positive equity. When total assets are less than total liabilities, a company has negative equity. A wonderful company should increase its equity every year.

A return on capital of 5% is an okay company. ROC is like interest rate, but different. A ROC of 5% is worse than bank CD paying 5% or a corporate bond paying 5%. A 5% CD is guaranteed by a bank and FDIC. The company guarantees a 5% corporate bond unless the bond is in default. A company can play accounting tricks to achieve a non-existing 5% ROC. For a higher risk by investing in equity, we ask for higher return.

A company that achieves ROC over 30% in the last 5 years or 10 years indicates the company has competitive advantages or a wide moat. A company can achieve competitive advantages through economic of scales, holding key patents, large distribution channels, legislative monopolies, high hardware or software switching costs, and dominant market shares (Dorsey, 2008).

Return on equity (ROE) is an important investment ratio. It equals the total net income of a company over a period, usually one year, divided by company's equity. You can easily find a company's ROE data. Return on capital takes the debt factor into the calculation, so Return on capital is a better measure than return on equity when comparing companies with different leverage ratios.

Leverage is a company's usage of debts to achieve higher ROE. For example, you can borrow money or use margins to trade or invest in stocks and stock options. In a good year, you can achieve higher return using debts. In a bad year, you can lose all your investment, and you still owe money to the brokerage firms or banks. Lehman Brothers' leverage ratio was 44 to 1 in 2007 (Bankruptcy of Lehman Brothers, 2013), and Bear Stearns' leverage ratio was 35 to 1 in 2008 (Boyd, 2008). The high leverage ratios brought down these two large financial institutions in 2008. Joel Greenblatt also prefers return on capital method in his book: The Little Book that Still Beats the Market (Greenblatt, 2010).

A company has some controls over accounting profits. Sometimes frauds are involved. People lost their investments, pensions, or even lifetime savings to Enron, WorldCom, and HealthSouth scandals. So it is important to check the cash flow statements. Cash is harder to manipulate. A company's Total Cash Flows from Operating Activities should increase year over year if its ROE are increasing 10% or more each year.

Revenue per Employee and Knowledge Economy

Samsung Group' annual revenues were $268.8 billion, and its net income was $26.2 billion in 2012. Samsung had 425,000 employees worldwide in 2012 (Samsung, 2013). The revenue per employee was $632,470.59 per employee. Samsung's 2012 revenues put it ahead the national GDP of Pakistan, Portugal, or New Zealand (IMF Report for Selected Countries and Subjects, 2013).

McDonald's revenue per employee for is $63,000, and its net income per employee is $12,500. Yum! Brands Company operates Taco Bell, KFC, and Pizza Hut worldwide. Yum!'s revenue per employee is $25,000; its income per employee is $2,100 (MSN Money Investing - Key Ratios, 2013). It is easy to understand why KFC's cashiers can only earn minimum wages. Comparing to Samsung's $632,000 per employee, you can see the wealth creation and income difference.

In summary, the Return on Capital of a wonderful company should be 20% or higher for last 5 years.

"Charlie and I look for companies that have a) a business we understand; b) favorable long-term economics; c) able and trustworthy management; and d) a sensible price tag." – Warren Buffett 2007

Chapter 3   Fair Prices

"Price is what you pay, value is what you get."-- Warren Buffett

"Ben [Graham] was right the market is a manic depressive. That's why you can't buy and sell on its terms. You have to buy and sell when you want to."-- Warren Buffett

Beginner investors may think that a stock costing $10/share is cheaper than another stock costing $90/share. It is not necessary to be true.

When you buy shares of stocks, you buy a piece of an incoming producing company. You should consider what the total company worth, or its market capitalization. A company's market capitalization equals to stock price/share times the total outstanding shares. The company has assets, liabilities, and net equity. Net equity is the amounts that value of assets is over the liabilities. To make money in stock market, what you need to do is to buy low, and sell high. You can buy low by a few methods.

One way to buy low is using Benjamin Graham's net nets method. In this method, you buy company stocks when liquid assets worth more than its liabilities. Graham called this margin of safety in his Intelligent Investor book. It was common during Graham's time to find such net nets companies because people could not find financial information easily. Today finding such companies is much harder.

Charlie Munger, Warren Buffett's partner, introduced him to buy See's candy. After See's purchase, they have been favoring an approach that buys a wonderful company at fair price focusing on its growth aspect. They focus less on a fair company at a wonderful price. Buffett called a fair company at a wonderful price a cigar butt, because of only one puff of smoke left. Buffett described himself as 15% Philip Fisher and 85% Benjamin

Graham. Philip Fisher was a growth investor. Philip Fisher is the father of Ken Fisher, a billionaire money manager.

Great and rapidly growing companies are usually not cheap, commanding sometimes very high P/E ratios, or with even negative P/E for early stage technology companies. P/E ratio is the market price per share divided by its annual net earnings per share. P/E is an important investment ratio. The median P/E ratio for S&P index companies is around 15. The lower the P/E, the cheaper a company stock is. On the other side, the higher the P/E, the more expensive the company stock is.

If we flip the Price/ Earnings ratio, it becomes Earnings / Price. Earnings/Price is called earning yield. Earnings yields are comparable to bank saving rates, CD interest rates, and government bond yields, and corporate bond yields. A stock equity earnings yields should be at least several points higher than US government bond yields because investors bear more risks of losing money.

The stock price of a company can become cheap when the whole stock market is depressed. Most technology stocks were down in 2002; most stocks were done in early 2009. Temporary company specific problems occasionally develop. As Warren Buffett stated, the stock market has a bipolar disorder. When the market is in a manic mood, no price is too high for a hot company. When the market is in a depressive mood, no price is too low for a beaten company. Mr. Market and margin of safety are the two most important concepts of Benjamin Graham's Intelligent Investor book.

Chapter 4 Emotional Intelligence, Mirror Neurons, and Contrarian Investors

"Be fearful when others are greedy, and greedy when others are fearful."-- Warren Buffett

"To invest successfully over a lifetime does not require a stratospheric IQ, unusual business insights, or inside information. What's needed is a sound intellectual framework for making decisions and the ability to keep emotions from corroding that framework. This book [The Intelligent Investor] precisely and clearly prescribes the proper framework. You must supply the emotional discipline."-- Warren Buffett

"There are five dangerous faults which may affect a general: (1) Recklessness, which leads to destruction; (2) cowardice, which leads to capture; (3) a hasty temper, which can be provoked by insults; (4) a delicacy of honor which is sensitive to shame; (5) over-solicitude for his men, which exposes him to worry and trouble." -- Sun Tzu's The Art of War

Until a few years ago, I was not aware the importance of emotional intelligence in our daily life and in successful investing. Our two daughters and one son are about 4 four years apart. My wife went back to college full time after our second child. My mother-in-law has been living with us to help with the kids. I sometimes have had difficulties dealing with my mother in law. Living in the same household with my in-law has been challenges at the beginning. My wife and I have had many arguments because of the in-laws. She wants her parents to live with us. I felt that my wife wanted to live with her parents more than to live with our children and me. At one point, the relationship became intense. We went to marriage counseling. We had wonderful counselors Ken and Jen. Ken told gave me many good advices and told me that successful people usually also had high emotional intelligence. I read a couple books on emotional intelligence:

Emotional Intelligence: Why It Can Matter More Than IQ, a classic by Daniel Goleman and Emotional Intelligence 2.0 by Travis Bradberry & Jean Greaves. Emotional Intelligence is known as EQ. It is believed that IQ contributes 20 percent to the factors that determine life success. EQ is twice as important as IQ in getting where you want to go in life (Bradberry & Greaves, 2009).

According Dr. Goleman, emotional intelligence includes abilities: (1) to motivate oneself and persist in the face of frustration; (2) to control impulse and delay gratification; (3) to regulate one's moods and keep distress from swamping the ability to think; and (4) to empathize and to hope. IQ has one-century history of research, but EQ is a new idea. While IQ cannot be changed much, EQ can be learned and improved through experience and education for children and adults (Goleman, Emotional Intelligence: Why It Can Matter More Than IQ , 2005).

Our brain has different systems. According to Paul MacLean, the following three distinct brains emerged successively in the course of evolution and now co-inhabit the human skull: the reptilian brain, the limbic brain, and the neocortex.

The reptilian brain, the oldest of the three, controls the body's vital functions such as heart rate, breathing, body temperature and balance. Our reptilian brain includes the main structures found in a reptile's brain: the brainstem and the cerebellum. The reptilian brain is reliable but tends to be somewhat rigid and compulsive. The limbic brain emerged in the first mammals. It can record memories of behaviors that produced agreeable and disagreeable experiences, so it is responsible for what are called emotions in human beings. The main structures of the limbic brain are the hippocampus, the amygdala, and the hypothalamus. The limbic brain is the seat of the value judgments that we make, often unconsciously, that exert such a strong influence on our behavior.

The neocortex first assumed importance in primates and culminated in the human brain with its two large cerebral hemispheres that play such a dominant role. These hemispheres have been responsible for the development of human language, abstract thought, imagination, and consciousness. The neocortex is flexible and has almost infinite learning abilities. The neocortex is also what has enabled human cultures to develop (The Evolutionary Layers of the Human Brain, 2013).

One key part of the limbic system is amygdala. Amygdala sometimes can get hijacked. During amygdala hijacking, your limbic system overtakes your logic-thinking cortex (Goleman, Emotional Intelligence: Why It Can Matter More Than IQ , 2005). That is why during heated arguments, people act on impulse and later regret. It is difficult to reason during heated moments, because the limbic system is in control. Limbic system, including amygdala, is less effective during our modern time. Limbic system can cause poor investment decisions.

Emotional brain, which including the limbic system, is important for people to make decisions. The limbic system ranks decisions or gives values to different possibilities subconsciously. Patients whose links between the neocortex, the thinking brain, and the emotional brain had been cut due to cancer surgeries could not make simple decisions while other normal brain functions are intact (Goleman, Emotional Intelligence: Why It Can Matter More Than IQ , 2005).

Our brain cannot do complicated spreadsheet calculations, which we will do in the next chapter. We cannot mentally rank 70 stocks with 6 columns of financial ratios. A formula with the help of Microsoft spreadsheet will do better a job. Our emotional brains use memories, love and hate emotional factors to rank possibilities. Such emotional decisions are often bad for investments. As Warren Buffett said, "I never buy anything unless I can fill out on a piece of paper my reasons. I may be wrong, but I would know the answer to that. "I'm paying $32 billion today for the Coca Cola Company because..." If you can't answer that question, you shouldn't buy it. If you can answer that question, and you do it a few times, you'll make a lot of money". When making investment decisions, you want thinking brain to supersede your emotional brain.

Dr. Coleman and Travis Bradberry recommended a few steps during highly stressful circumstances. First, stop at this red light. Second, breathe deeply, and take a short break, or take a walk. Calm down your limbic system. Let your thinking cortex brain take control. Plan about strategies/solutions to proceed. Finally, when the light turns green, you can go ahead. You can use these simple steps when you get an urge to buy and sell securities.

Have you ever wondered that why you did not take advantages when the stocks prices were low after the dot.com bubble in 2001 and financial crisis in early 2009? It is hard to be a contrarian against the crowd. The herd mentality has something to do with mirror neurons in our brains. Human emotions such as fears, joys, sadness, and angers are contagious. In early 1990s, scientists discovered mirror neurons in human and certain animals' brains (NOVA, 2005). Mirror neurons "mirror" the behaviors of others as if the observers were acting themselves. For example, when you watch someone yawning or licking an ice cream, you automatically start to yawn or to lick your mouth.

Daniel Goleman called these mirror neurons neural Wi-Fi in his book: Social Intelligence – The Revolutionary New Science of Human Relationships. "Mirror" neurons do just that: they reflect back an action we observe in someone else, making us to mimic that action or have the impulse to do so (Goleman, Social Intelligence: The New Science of Human Relationships, 2007). If we have tired arms, and when you watched a woman is massaging a man's arms, you will feel better for our own arms. Our mirror neurons send signals to our arms. But, we know that the massaged arms are not ours because our nerve sensors in our arms veto these nerve signals. Dr. Vilayanur S. Ramachandran of University of California found that people with amputated limbs would feel like the woman is actually massaging their arms because of no arm sensory nerves to veto the neuron signals. When an arm or leg is amputated, patients often continue to feel vividly the presence of the missing limb as a "phantom limb". 60 to 80 percent of individuals with an amputation experience phantom sensations in their amputated limb, and the majority of the sensations are painful. Dr. Ramachandran developed a mirror box to successfully treat phantom limb pains (Vilayanur S. Ramachandran, 2013).

Human has multiple mirror neuron systems. Mirror Neurons are not just for mimicking actions, but also for reading intentions, empathizing, language learning, and children general learning. Psychiatrist Daniel Stern of University of Geneva explained that: "our nervous systems are constructed to be captured by the nervous systems of others, so that we can experience others as if from within their skin" (Stern, 2004). "See our minds as so independent, but instead we must view them as "permeable" (Goleman, Social Intelligence: The New Science of Human Relationships, 2007). At a subconscious level, we continuously dialogue with anyone we interact with, our every feeling and every way of moving in tune to theirs.

Giancomo Rizzolatti, who discovered mirror neurons, explains, these systems "allow us to grasp the minds of others not through conceptual reasoning but through direct simulation; by feeling, not by thinking" (Goleman, Social Intelligence: The New Science of Human Relationships, 2007). We cannot function without conceptual reasoning or analogical reasoning. As Elon Musk of Tesla Motors said "I think it's important to reason from first principles rather than by analogy…The normal way we conduct our lives is we reason by analogy". "First principles" is a physics way of looking at the world…what that really means is that you boil things down to the most fundamental truths…and then reason up from there…that takes a lot more mental energy."

To invest successfully, you need to do more your independent physics way of thinking, and less analogical way of thinking. One way of physics way of investment thinking is to find the fundamental elements of facts, to select stocks through ranking them, and to create a formula.

"An investor will succeed by coupling good business judgment with an ability to insulate his thoughts and behavior from the super-contagious emotions that swirl about the marketplace. In my own efforts to stay insulated, I have found it highly useful to keep Ben's Mr. Market concept firmly in mind." -- Warren Buffett

Chapter 5   the Formula

"Everything should be made as simple as possible, but not simpler." -- Albert Einstein

"Now the general who wins a battle makes many calculations in his temple before the battle is fought. The general who loses a battle makes but few calculations beforehand. Thus do many calculations lead to victory and few calculations to defeat: how much more no calculation at all! It is by attention to this point that I can foresee who is likely to win or lose." -- Sun Tzu's The Art of War

Before you decide which stocks to buy, it is best to rank the stocks and pick the best stocks. Here are these simple steps:

Step 1:   Picking your great people.

Time's the World's 100 Most Influential People have the most weights. For example Mark Zuckerberg was on the list of Time 100 in 2008, 2011, and Time 100 All Time. He is ranked 2nd on the People Ranking Category. The more times that a person is on Time 100 over the last 10 years, the higher he or she ranks. After Time 100, the ranking orders are the key person(s) appear(s) on the list of both Barron's Best CEOs and Harvard Business Review's 100 Best Performing CEOs in the World. If the person appears only on one magazine, I count the times of appearance. You do not need a huge list; you only need a best list. I value the people element three times more important than other elements. So I multiply the element by 3. Give the company with the lowest people rank a score of 1. A company ranked 8th gets a score of 3 x 8 = 24, and so on.

Step 2:   Rank these companies by 5 Year or Life Average Sales Growth Rate, the higher the better. If the Life of the public company is less than 5 year, I use the life average sales growth rate. I value the 5 Year or Life Average Sales Growth Rate factor twice more important than other factors, so the ranking is multiplied by a factor of 2.

Step 3:   Rank these companies by 5 Year or Life Average Return on Capital, the higher the better. I value the 5 Year or Life Average Return on Capital factor the same important than other factors, so the ranking is multiplied by a factor of 1.

Step 4:   Rank these companies by the most recent 1 Year Return on Capital, the higher the better. I value the 1 Year Return on Capital factor the same important than other factors, so the ranking is multiplied by a factor of 1.

Step 5:   Rank these companies by the $Revenue per Employee, the higher the better. I value the $Revenue per Employee factor the same important than other factors, so the ranking is multiplied by a factor of 1.

Step 6:   Rank cheap companies using P/E ratio or Earning Yield.

Lower P/E is ranked higher. If you use Earning Yield (the reverse of P/E), higher Earning Yield is ranked higher. Rank the companies using the sort function from low to high if you use the P/E. Note you should take companies with negative P/E out of the rankings, and treat them differently. Use the forward P/E instead of the trailing P/E for companies with negative trailing P/E. Rank the companies from high to low if you use the Earning Yield percentage. I value the P/E ratio factor the same important than other factors, so the ranking is multiplied by a factor of 1. Give the company with the lowest P/E a score of 1. A company ranked 8th gets a score of 8, and so on.

Step 7: Combine the scores of the six lists. Sort the companies from low to high by the combined scores. The lowest score company is our number one choice. That means a wonderful company (high ROC, 5 Year Average Return on Capital, 1 Year Return on Capital and $Revenue per Employee) and fair price (low P/E) with a proven world business leader.

Below I give an example on how I screen, sort, and rank companies to arrive final scores using a 76 companies based on October 3, 2013 data.

Step 1: Picking your people.

People Rank scores equal to the ranking number times 3.

Company Name	Key Person(s)	Magazine (T – Time of appearances)	People Ranking	Score 3x
JP Morgan Chase (JPM)	Jamie Dimon	Time 2011, 2009, 2008, and 2006; Barron's 2013, 2012, 2011, 2010, & 2009 (4T)	1	3
Facebook, Inc. (FB)	Mark Zuckerberg	Time 2011, 2008 & All Time (3T)	2	6
Google Inc. (GOOG)	Lawrence Page, Sergrey Brin & Kevin	Time 2013, 2011 & 2004; Barron's	3	9

	Systrom (Instagram)	2013 (3T)		
Amazon.com Inc. (AMZN)	Jeffrey Bezos	Time 2009 & 2008; Barron's 2013, 2012, 2011, 2010 & 2009; HBR 2013 (2T)	4	12
Netflix (NFLX)	Reed Hastings	Time 2011 and 2005; Barron's 2011, 2010, & 2009 (2T)	5	15
Cisco Systems, Inc. (CSCO)	John T. Chambers	Time 2008 & 2004; Barron's 2010, 2008; HBR 2013 (2T)	6	18
SolarCity Corporation (SCTY)	Elon Musk	Time 2013, 2010 (2T)	7	21
Tesla Mortors, Inc. (TSLA)	Elon Musk	Time 2013, 2010 (2T)	7	21
Berkshire Hathaway (BRK.A)	Warren Buffett	Time 2008; Barron's 2013, 2012, 2011, 2010 2009 & 2008 (1T+6)	9	27
Costoco Wholesale (COST)	Jim Sinegal	Time 2006; Barron's 2011, 2010, 2009 & 2008 (1T +4)	10	30

Company	CEO	Source		
Fast Retailing (FRCOY)	Tadashi Yanai	Time 2013; Barron's 2013 & 2012 (1T+2)	11	33
Starbucks Corporation (SBUX)	Howard Schultz	Time 2004; Barron's 2013, 2012 (1T+2)	11	33
Wynn Resorts (WYNN)	Steve Wynn	Time 2006; Barron's 2011 & 2009 (1T+2)	11	33
ArcelorMittal (MT)	Lakshmi Mittal	Time 2008; Barron's 2008 (1T+1)	14	42
General Electric (GE)	Jeffrey Immelt	Time 2008; Barron's 2008 (1T+1)	14	42
Samsung Elect Ltd (F) (SSNLF)	Lee Kun-hee & Yun Jong-yong	Time 2005; HBR 2013 (1T+1)	14	42
Apple Inc. (AAPL)	Timothy Cook	Time 2012 (1T+0)	17	51
Baidu, Inc. (BIDU)	Robin Yanhong Li	Time 2010 (1T+0)	17	51
Michael Kors Holdings Limited (KORS)	Michael Kors	Time 2013 (1T+0)	17	51
Yahoo! Inc. (YHOO)	Marissa A. Mayer	Time 2013(T+0)	17	51
Coach, Inc. (COH)	Lew Frankfort	Barron's 2012 & 2008; HBR 2013 (B&H)	21	63
EOG Resources (EOG)	Mark Papa	Barron's 2010; HBR 2013 (B&H)	21	63

Company	CEO	Source		
Fomento Economico Mexicano (FMX)	Jose Carbajal	Barron's 2013; HBR 2013 (B&H)	21	63
Monsanto Company (MON)	Hugh Grant	Barron's 2008; HBR 2013 (B&H)	21	63
Novo Nordisk A/S (NVO)	Lars Rebien S.	Barron's 2013; HBR 2013 (B&H)	21	63
Simon Property Group Inc. (SPG)	David Simon	Barron's 2013; HBR 2013 (B&H)	21	63
Tesco (TESO)	Terry Leahy	Barron's 2010 & 2008; HBR 2013 (B&H)	21	63
Yum! Brands (YUM)	David Novak	Barron's 2013, 2011 & 2009; HBR 2013 (B&H)	21	63
BlackRock (BLK)	Larry Fink	Barron's 2013, 2012, 2011, 2010, 2009 & 2008 (6B)	29	87
FedEx (FDX)	Fred Smith	Barron's 2013, 2012, 2011, 2010, 2009 & 2008 (6B)	29	87
Abbott Laboratories (ABT)	Miles White	Barron's 2013, 2012, 2011, 2010 & 2009 (5B)	31	93
Anheuser-Busch InBev (BUD)	Carlos Brito	Barron's 2013, 2011 & 2009 (4B)	32	96

Company	CEO	Source		
Canon (CAJ)	Fujio Mitarai	Barron's 2011, 20110, 2009 & 2008 (4B)	32	96
ExxonMobile (XOM)	Rex Tillerson	Barron's 2012, 2011 2010 & 2009 (4B)	32	96
Ford Motor Company (F)	Alan Mulally	Barron's 2013, 2012, 2010 & 2009 (4B)	32	96
IBM (IBM)	Sam Palmisano	Barron's 2011, 2010, 2009 & 2008 (4B)	32	96
Oracle Corporation (ORCL)	Larry Ellison	Barron's 2013, 2011, 2010, 2009 (4B)	32	96
ARM Holdings (ARMH)	Warren East	Barron's 2013, 2011 & 2009 (3B)	37	111
BHP Billiton (BHP)	Marius Kloppers	Barron's 2012, 2011 & 2009 (3B)	37	111
EMC (EMC)	Joe Tucci	Barron's 2012, 2011 & 2009 (3B)	37	111
McDonald's (MCD)	Jim Skinner	Barron's 2012, 2010 & 2009 (3B)	37	111
TD Bank Group (TD)	Ed Clark	Barron's 2013, 2012 & 2008 (3B)	37	111
Hewlett Packard (HPQ)	Mark Hurd	Barron's 2010 & 2008 (2B)	42	126

Siemens (SI)	Peter Loscher	Barron's 2012 & 2011 (2B)	42	126
Allergan Inc. (AGN)	David Pyott	HBR 2013 (1)	44	132
America Movil (AMX)	Daniel Abounmrad	HBR 2013 (1H)	44	132
American Express (AXP)	Kenneth Chenault	Barron's 2008 (1)	44	132
BYD (BYD)	Wang Chuan-fu	Barron's 2010 (1B)	44	132
CBS (CBS)	Leslie Moonres	Barron's 2013 (1)	44	132
Deere & Co. (DE)	Robert Lane	Barron's 2008 (1)	44	132
Dish Network (DISH)	Charlie Ergen	Barron's (1B)	44	132
Enbridge (ENB)	Patrick Daniel	HBR 2013 (1)	44	132
Expeditors Int'l (EXPD)	Peter Rose	Barron's 2008 (1B)	44	132
Express Scripts (ESRX)	George Paz	HBR 2013 (1)	44	132
Gilead Sciences, Inc. (GILD)	John Martin	HBR 2013 (1)	44	132
Group Danone (DANOY)	Frank Riboud	Barron's 2008 (1)	44	132
Honeywell (HON)	David Cote	Barron's 2013 (1)	44	132
Intel (INTC)	Paul Otellini	Barron's 2012 (1B)	44	132
Nordstrom (JWN)	Blake Nordstrom	HBR 2013 (1)	44	132
Perrigo (PRGO)	Joseph Papa	Barron's 2012 (1)	44	132
Petrobras (PZE)	Jose Gobrielli	Barron's 2010 (1B)	44	132

Potash Corp. (POT)	William Doyle	HBR 2013 (1)	44	132
Precision Castparts (PCP)	Mark Donegan	HBR 2013 (1)	44	132
Priceline.com (PCLN)	Jeffrey Boyd	Barron's 2012 (1)	44	132
Procter & Gamble (PG)	A.G. Lafley	Barron's 2008 (1)	44	132
Royal Bank of Canada (RY)	Gordon Nixon	Barron's 2011 (1)	44	132
Royal Bank of Scotland (RBS)	Fred Goodwin	Barron's 2008 (1)	44	132
Ryanair Holdings (RYAAY)	Michael O'Leary	Barron's 2013 (1)	44	132
SABMiller (SBMRY)	Graham Mckay	HBR 2013 (1)	44	132
Salesforce.com (CRM)	Marc Benioff	Barron's 2012 (1)	44	132
SAP (SAP.AG)	Kenning Kagermann	Barron's 2008 (1)	44	132
Sherwin-Williams (SHW)	Christopher Connor	HBR 2013 (1)	44	132
Swatch Group (SWGAY)	Hugh Hayek	Barron's 2013 (1)	44	132
Taiwan Semiconductor (TSM)	Morris Chang	Barron's 2013 (1)	44	132
Tenaris (TS)	Paolo Rocca	HBR 2013 (1)	44	132
TJX (TJX)	Carol Meyrowitz	Barron's 2013 (1)	44	132

T: Time; B: Barron's; and H: Harvard Business Review

Step 2: Rank these companies by 5 Year or Life Average Sales Growth Rate, the higher the better.

Multiply the ranking number by 2 to arrive the 5 Year or Life Average Sales Growth Rate score.

Company Name	5 Year or Life Sales Growth Ave.	5 Year or Life Sales Growth Ave. Ranking	5 Year or Life Sales Growth Ave. Score 2x
Tesla Mortors, Inc. (TSLA)	463.09	1	2
Baidu, Inc. (BIDU)	66.43	2	4
Michael Kors Holdings Limited (KORS)	54.50	3	6
Facebook, Inc. (FB)	53.10	4	8
Apple Inc. (AAPL)	45.49	5	10
Express Scripts (ESRX)	38.72	6	12
Amazon.com Inc. (AMZN)	32.72	7	14
Salesforce.com (CRM)	32.44	8	16
Priceline.com (PCLN)	30.14	9	18
Google Inc. (GOOG)	24.77	10	20

Netflix (NFLX)	24.53	11	22
EOG Resources (EOG)	23.67	12	24
America Movil (AMX)	19.88	13	26
Gilead Sciences, Inc. (GILD)	18.06	14	28
ARM Holdings (ARMH)	17.33	15	30
Enbridge (ENB)	16.25	16	32
BYD (BYD)	15.91	17	34
Samsung Electronics Ltd (F) (SSNLF)	15.34	18	36
Perrigo (PRGO)	14.20	19	38
BlackRock (BLK)	14.02	20	40
Wynn Resorts (WYNN)	13.91	21	42
Anheuser-Busch InBev (BUD)	13.57	22	44
Novo Nordisk A/S (NVO)	13.25	23	46

Ryanair Holdings (RYAAY)	12.47	24	48
Fast Retailing (FRCOY)	12.07	25	50
Oracle Corporation (ORCL)	10.64	26	52
EMC (EMC)	10.42	27	54
Group Danone (DANOY)	10.31	28	56
Fomento Economico Mexicano (FMX)	10.14	29	58
Coach, Inc. (COH)	9.80	30	60
TD Bank Group (TD)	9.68	31	62
SAP (SAP.AG)	9.60	32	64
Taiwan Semiconductor (TSM)	9.43	33	66
Abbott Laboratories (ABT)	9.00	34	68
Deere & Co. (DE)	8.74	35	70
Potash Corp. (POT)	8.66	36	72
Allergan Inc. (AGN)	8.07	37	74

Costoco Wholesale (COST)	7.73	38	76
Starbucks Corporation (SBUX)	7.16	39	78
Intel (INTC)	6.83	40	80
TJX (TJX)	6.77	41	82
Swatch Group (SWGAY)	6.67	42	84
Nordstrom (JWN)	6.59	43	86
Berkshire Hathaway (BRK.A)	6.56	44	88
JP Morgan Chase (JPM)	6.34	45	90
Simon Property Group Inc. (SPG)	5.98	46	92
Yum! Brands (YUM)	5.53	47	94
Monsanto Company (MON)	5.51	48	96
Dish Network (DISH)	5.17	49	98
Cisco Systems, Inc. (CSCO)	4.22	50	100
Precision Castparts (PCP)	4.10	51	102
Royal Bank of Canada (RY)	4.00	52	104

McDonald's (MCD)	3.88	53	106
Tesco (TESO)	3.65	54	108
ExxonMobile (XOM)	3.58	55	110
Sherwin-Williams (SHW)	3.56	56	112
FedEx (FDX)	3.14	57	114
Hewlett Packard (HPQ)	2.91	58	116
Expeditors Int'l (EXPD)	2.70	59	118
American Express (AXP)	2.63	60	120
BHP Billiton (BHP)	1.87	61	122
Honeywell (HON)	1.72	62	124
SABMiller (SBMRY)	1.63	63	126
Siemens (SI)	1.56	64	128
Tenaris (TS)	1.53	65	130
IBM (IBM)	1.13	66	132
Procter & Gamble (PG)	0.16	67	134
CBS (CBS)	0.02	68	136
Petrobras (PZE)	(1.06)	69	138
General Electric (GE)	(3.13)	70	140

Company Name			
ArcelorMittal (MT)	(4.36)	71	142
Ford Motor Company (F)	(4.89)	72	144
Canon (CAJ)	(5.00)	73	146
Yahoo! Inc. (YHOO)	(6.48)	74	148
Royal Bank of Scotland (RBS)	(9.61)	75	150
SolarCity Corporation (SCTY)	(18.50)	76	152

Step 3: Rank wonderful companies using 5 Year or Life Average Return on Capital, the higher the better.

Company Name	5 Year or Life Average Return on Capital	5 Year or Life Average Return on Capital Ranking	5 Year or Life Average Return on Capital Score
Michael Kors Holdings Limited (KORS)	51.47	1	1
Coach, Inc. (COH)	48.50	2	2
Baidu, Inc. (BIDU)	43.80	3	3
TJX (TJX)	36.40	4	4
Novo Nordisk A/S (NVO)	36.10	5	5
Apple Inc. (AAPL)	35.70	6	6

Priceline.com (PCLN)	29.70	7	7
Gilead Sciences, Inc. (GILD)	29.60	8	8
IBM (IBM)	27.80	9	9
ExxonMobile (XOM)	24.50	10	10
Yum! Brands (YUM)	23.30	11	11
Taiwan Semiconductor (TSM)	22.00	12	12
Potash Corp. (POT)	21.60	13	13
Netflix (NFLX)	20.90	14	14
SAP (SAP.AG)	19.50	15	15
Expeditors Int'l (EXPD)	19.50	16	16
Sherwin-Williams (SHW)	18.80	17	17
Starbucks Corporation (SBUX)	18.70	18	18
BHP Billiton (BHP)	18.40	19	19
Fast Retailing (FRCOY)	18.20	20	20

McDonald's (MCD)	18.00	21	21
Intel (INTC)	18.00	22	22
Google Inc. (GOOG)	17.60	23	23
America Movil (AMX)	16.80	24	24
Precision Castparts (PCP)	16.10	25	25
Swatch Group (SWGAY)	15.90	26	26
Oracle Corporation (ORCL)	15.40	27	27
Express Scripts (ESRX)	14.50	28	28
Samsung Electronics Ltd (F) (SSNLF)	14.40	29	29
Monsanto Company (MON)	13.50	30	30
Amazon.com Inc. (AMZN)	12.90	31	31
Abbott Laboratories (ABT)	12.80	32	32
Tenaris (TS)	12.30	33	33
Cisco Systems, Inc. (CSCO)	12.20	34	34
Honeywell (HON)	12.10	35	35

Company			
Procter & Gamble (PG)	11.60	36	36
Yahoo! Inc. (YHOO)	11.20	37	37
Fomento Economico Mexicano (FMX)	11.00	38	38
Costoco Wholesale (COST)	10.70	39	39
Perrigo (PRGO)	10.70	40	40
Nordstrom (JWN)	10.60	41	41
ARM Holdings (ARMH)	9.70	42	42
Allergan Inc. (AGN)	9.20	43	43
Group Danone (DANOY)	9.10	44	44
EMC (EMC)	9.00	45	45
Canon (CAJ)	8.60	46	46
EOG Resources (EOG)	7.60	47	47
Siemens (SI)	7.50	48	48
FedEx (FDX)	7.20	49	49
BYD (BYD)	6.90	50	50
SABMiller (SBMRY)	6.40	51	51
BlackRock (BLK)	6.30	52	52

Company			
Hewlett Packard (HPQ)	6.10	53	53
Tesco (TESO)	6.00	54	54
Deere & Co. (DE)	4.80	55	55
Berkshire Hathaway (BRK.A)	4.30	56	56
Facebook, Inc. (FB)	3.63	57	57
Ryanair Holdings (RYAAY)	3.30	58	58
Ford Motor Company (F)	2.88	59	59
Enbridge (ENB)	2.80	60	60
Anheuser-Busch InBev (BUD)	2.50	61	61
Petrobras (PZE)	2.30	62	62
American Express (AXP)	2.10	63	63
Wynn Resorts (WYNN)	1.80	64	64
Salesforce.com (CRM)	1.00	65	65
ArcelorMittal (MT)	0.40	66	66
JP Morgan Chase (JPM)	0.10	67	67
General Electric (GE)	(0.30)	68	68
Simon Property Group Inc. (SPG)	(1.20)	69	69
Dish Network (DISH)	(2.31)	70	70

Company Name		Ranking	Score
TD Bank Group (TD)	(4.70)	71	71
Royal Bank of Canada (RY)	(5.60)	72	72
CBS (CBS)	(7.80)	73	73
Royal Bank of Scotland (RBS)	(8.00)	74	74
Tesla Mortors, Inc. (TSLA)	(27.88)	75	75
SolarCity Corporation (SCTY)	(28.41)	76	76

Step 4: Rank wonderful companies using Most Recent 1 Year Return on Capital, the higher the better.

Company Name	1 Year or Life Average Return on Capital	1 Year or Life Average Return on Capital Ranking	1 Year or Life Average Return on Capital Score
Michael Kors Holdings Limited (KORS)	51.47	1	1
Coach, Inc. (COH)	48.50	2	2
Baidu, Inc. (BIDU)	43.80	3	3
TJX (TJX)	36.40	4	4
Novo Nordisk A/S (NVO)	36.10	5	5
Apple Inc. (AAPL)	35.70	6	6
Priceline.com (PCLN)	29.70	7	7

Gilead Sciences, Inc. (GILD)	29.60	8	8
IBM (IBM)	27.80	9	9
ExxonMobile (XOM)	24.50	10	10
Yum! Brands (YUM)	23.30	11	11
Taiwan Semiconductor (TSM)	22.00	12	12
Potash Corp. (POT)	21.60	13	13
Netflix (NFLX)	20.90	14	14
SAP (SAP.AG)	19.50	15	15
Expeditors Int'l (EXPD)	19.50	16	16
Sherwin-Williams (SHW)	18.80	17	17
Starbucks Corporation (SBUX)	18.70	18	18
BHP Billiton (BHP)	18.40	19	19
Fast Retailing (FRCOY)	18.20	20	20
McDonald's (MCD)	18.00	21	21
Intel (INTC)	18.00	22	22
Google Inc. (GOOG)	17.60	23	23
America Movil (AMX)	16.80	24	24
Precision Castparts (PCP)	16.10	25	25

Swatch Group (SWGAY)	15.90	26	26
Oracle Corporation (ORCL)	15.40	27	27
Express Scripts (ESRX)	14.50	28	28
Samsung Electronics Ltd (F) (SSNLF)	14.40	29	29
Monsanto Company (MON)	13.50	30	30
Amazon.com Inc. (AMZN)	12.90	31	31
Abbott Laboratories (ABT)	12.80	32	32
Tenaris (TS)	12.30	33	33
Cisco Systems, Inc. (CSCO)	12.20	34	34
Honeywell (HON)	12.10	35	35
Procter & Gamble (PG)	11.60	36	36
Yahoo! Inc. (YHOO)	11.20	37	37
Fomento Economico Mexicano (FMX)	11.00	38	38
Costoco Wholesale (COST)	10.70	39	39
Perrigo (PRGO)	10.70	40	40
Nordstrom (JWN)	10.60	41	41
ARM Holdings (ARMH)	9.70	42	42
Allergan Inc. (AGN)		43	43

	9.20		
Group Danone (DANOY)	9.10	44	44
EMC (EMC)	9.00	45	45
Canon (CAJ)	8.60	46	46
EOG Resources (EOG)	7.60	47	47
Siemens (SI)	7.50	48	48
FedEx (FDX)	7.20	49	49
BYD (BYD)	6.90	50	50
SABMiller (SBMRY)	6.40	51	51
BlackRock (BLK)	6.30	52	52
Hewlett Packard (HPQ)	6.10	53	53
Tesco (TESO)	6.00	54	54
Deere & Co. (DE)	4.80	55	55
Berkshire Hathaway (BRK.A)	4.30	56	56
Facebook, Inc. (FB)	3.63	57	57
Ryanair Holdings (RYAAY)	3.30	58	58
Ford Motor Company (F)	2.88	59	59
Enbridge (ENB)	2.80	60	60
Anheuser-Busch InBev (BUD)	2.50	61	61
Petrobras (PZE)		62	62

		2.30		
American Express (AXP)		2.10	63	63
Wynn Resorts (WYNN)		1.80	64	64
Salesforce.com (CRM)		1.00	65	65
ArcelorMittal (MT)		0.40	66	66
JP Morgan Chase (JPM)		0.10	67	67
General Electric (GE)		(0.30)	68	68
Simon Property Group Inc. (SPG)		(1.20)	69	69
Dish Network (DISH)		(2.31)	70	70
TD Bank Group (TD)		(4.70)	71	71
Royal Bank of Canada (RY)		(5.60)	72	72
CBS (CBS)		(7.80)	73	73
Royal Bank of Scotland (RBS)		(8.00)	74	74
Tesla Mortors, Inc. (TSLA)		(27.88)	75	75
SolarCity Corporation (SCTY)		(28.41)	76	76

Step 5: Rank wonderful companies using US$ Revenue per Employee (Management Efficiency), the higher the better.

Company Name	$ Revenue per Employee (Management Efficiency) MSN Money	$ Revenue per Employee Rank	$ Revenue per Employee Rank Score 1x
Fast Retailing (FRCOY)	56,800,000.00	1	1
Canon (CAJ)	17,810,000.00	2	2
Taiwan Semiconductor (TSM)	14,290,000.00	3	3
ExxonMobile (XOM)	5,800,000.00	4	4
EOG Resources (EOG)	4,970,000.00	5	5
America Movil (AMX)	4,910,000.00	6	6
Petrobras (PZE)	4,630,000.00	7	7
Enbridge (ENB)	3,680,000.00	8	8
Express Scripts (ESRX)	3,500,000.00	9	9
Fomento Economico Mexicano (FMX)	2,440,000.00	10	10
Novo Nordisk A/S (NVO)	2,280,000.00	11	11

Apple Inc. (AAPL)	2,230,000.00	12	12
Gilead Sciences, Inc. (GILD)	2,060,000.00	13	13
Netflix (NFLX)	1,620,000.00	14	14
Potash Corp. (POT)	1,390,000.00	15	15
BHP Billiton (BHP)	1,330,000.00	16	16
Facebook, Inc. (FB)	1,320,000.00	17	17
Baidu, Inc. (BIDU)	1,250,000.00	18	18
Google Inc. (GOOG)	1,240,000.00	19	19
BlackRock (BLK)	932,380.95	20	20
Simon Property Group Inc. (SPG)	913,576.36	21	21
Samsung Electronics Ltd (F) (SSNLF)	840,409.85	22	22
Ford Motor Company (F)	833,339.18	23	23
Amazon.com Inc. (AMZN)	756,199.10	24	24
CBS (CBS)	702,484.47	25	25
Procter & Gamble (PG)	695,595.04	26	26

Company	Value		
Cisco Systems, Inc. (CSCO)	647,670.19	27	27
Priceline.com (PCLN)	618,863.16	28	28
Berkshire Hathaway (BRK.A)	604,263.43	29	29
Costoco Wholesale (COST)	571,500.00	30	30
Deere & Co. (DE)	570,052.32	31	31
Monsanto Company (MON)	567,213.74	32	32
Allergan Inc. (AGN)	541,553.57	33	33
Ryanair Holdings (RYAAY)	540,910.58	34	34
American Express (AXP)	506,393.70	35	35
Intel (INTC)	498,333.33	36	36
General Electric (GE)	478,737.70	37	37
Tesla Mortors, Inc. (TSLA)	446,480.09	38	38
Abbott Laboratories (ABT)	440,668.66	39	39
Expeditors Int'l (EXPD)	436,172.19	40	40
Yahoo! Inc. (YHOO)	412,235.13	41	41
Tenaris (TS)	409,506.39	42	42
Dish Network (DISH)	407,834.69	43	43
JP Morgan Chase		44	44

(JPM)	382,800.76		
Michael Kors Holdings Limited (KORS)	377,445.68	45	45
EMC (EMC)	371,815.03	46	46
Perrigo (PRGO)	357,555.56	47	47
Salesforce.com (CRM)	354,367.96	48	48
Royal Bank of Canada (RY)	349,687.50	49	49
Hewlett Packard (HPQ)	340,946.35	50	50
Wynn Resorts (WYNN)	331,156.63	51	51
SABMiller (SBMRY)	329,327.81	52	52
ArcelorMittal (MT)	326,367.77	53	53
Oracle Corporation (ORCL)	311,425.00	54	54
Precision Castparts (PCP)	308,028.07	55	55
TD Bank Group (TD)	303,646.82	56	56
Coach, Inc. (COH)	295,080.81	57	57
Honeywell (HON)	289,765.15	58	58
Sherwin-Williams (SHW)	284,187.88	59	59
FedEx (FDX)	277,031.74	60	60

Company	Value		
Swatch Group (SWGAY)	272,660.13	61	61
Anheuser-Busch InBev (BUD)	268,746.67	62	62
BYD (BYD)	258,058.44	63	63
ARM Holdings (ARMH)	255,459.54	64	64
SAP (SAP.AG)	253,265.92	65	65
Tesco (TESO)	250,172.68	66	66
IBM (IBM)	219,237.89	67	67
Group Danone (DANOY)	209,490.14	68	68
Nordstrom (JWN)	204,295.08	69	69
Siemens (SI)	190,495.05	70	70
Royal Bank of Scotland (RBS)	168,682.93	71	71
TJX (TJX)	149,534.97	72	72
Starbucks Corporation (SBUX)	90,383.13	73	73
McDonald's (MCD)	63,167.27	74	74
SolarCity Corporation (SCTY)	49,874.10	75	75
Yum! Brands (YUM)	24,967.50	76	76

Step 6: Rank cheap companies using Price / Earning Ratio (or P/E Ratio), the lower the better, except negative numbers.

Company Name	P/E	P/E Ranking	P/E Score 1x
Samsung Electronics Ltd (F) (SSNLF)	7.42	1	1
Petrobras (PZE)	8.14	2	2
Deere & Co. (DE)	9.59	3	3
ExxonMobile (XOM)	11.07	4	4
Ford Motor Company (F)	11.59	5	5
America Movil (AMX)	11.71	6	6
JP Morgan Chase (JPM)	11.89	7	7
Cisco Systems, Inc. (CSCO)	12.07	8	8
Potash Corp. (POT)	12.09	9	9
Royal Bank of Canada (RY)	12.09	10	10
IBM (IBM)	12.25	11	11
TD Bank Group (TD)	12.83	12	12
Anheuser-Busch InBev (BUD)	13.02	13	13
Apple Inc. (AAPL)	13.11	14	14

Intel (INTC)	13.11	15	15
Canon (CAJ)	13.25	16	16
Coach, Inc. (COH)	13.82	17	17
Oracle Corporation (ORCL)	14.25	18	18
Taiwan Semiconductor (TSM)	15.39	19	19
Nordstrom (JWN)	15.66	20	20
ArcelorMittal (MT)	16.01	21	21
Berkshire Hathaway (BRK.A)	16.14	22	22
Tesco (TESO)	16.32	23	23
McDonald's (MCD)	17.11	24	24
Tenaris (TS)	17.22	25	25
BHP Billiton (BHP)	17.66	26	26
TJX (TJX)	18.22	27	27
Siemens (SI)	18.25	28	28
EMC (EMC)	18.84	29	29
BlackRock (BLK)	19.29	30	30

General Electric (GE)	19.46	31	31
American Express (AXP)	19.54	32	32
Abbott Laboratories (ABT)	19.71	33	33
Group Danone (DANOY)	20.14	34	34
Ryanair Holdings (RYAAY)	20.48	35	35
Swatch Group (SWGAY)	20.49	36	36
Procter & Gamble (PG)	20.73	37	37
Fomento Economico Mexicano (FMX)	20.98	38	38
Honeywell (HON)	21.63	39	39
CBS (CBS)	22.56	40	40
Monsanto Company (MON)	23.48	41	41
Novo Nordisk A/S (NVO)	23.69	42	42
Precision Castparts (PCP)	24.62	43	43
SAP (SAP.AG)	24.75	44	44
Costoco Wholesale (COST)	25.15	45	45
SABMiller (SBMRY)	25.87	46	46
FedEx (FDX)	26.45	47	47
Google Inc. (GOOG)	27.62	48	48

Company	Value		
Expeditors Int'l (EXPD)	27.79	49	49
Yahoo! Inc. (YHOO)	27.83	50	50
Yum! Brands (YUM)	27.89	51	51
Perrigo (PRGO)	27.91	52	52
Express Scripts (ESRX)	28.00	53	53
Allergan Inc. (AGN)	29.86	54	54
Sherwin-Williams (SHW)	30.16	55	55
Wynn Resorts (WYNN)	30.57	56	56
Fast Retailing (FRCOY)	30.60	57	57
Baidu, Inc. (BIDU)	33.32	58	58
Michael Kors Holdings Limited (KORS)	34.07	59	59
Priceline.com (PCLN)	35.21	60	60
Starbucks Corporation (SBUX)	38.28	61	61
Gilead Sciences, Inc. (GILD)	38.99	62	62
Simon Property Group Inc. (SPG)	41.28	63	63
Enbridge (ENB)	52.78	64	64
EOG Resources (EOG)	67.02	65	65
Dish Network (DISH)	86.45	66	66

ARM Holdings (ARMH)	95.71	67	67
Tesla Mortors, Inc. (TSLA)	98.64	68	68
Amazon.com Inc. (AMZN)	129.32	69	69
BYD (BYD)	150.76	70	70
Facebook, Inc. (FB)	235.07	71	71
Netflix (NFLX)	408.51	71	71
Royal Bank of Scotland (RBS)	(8.40)	73	73
Salesforce.com (CRM)	(13.90)	74	74
SolarCity Corporation (SCTY)	(28.41)	75	75
Hewlett Packard (HPQ)	(41.40)	76	76

Step 7:   Combine the scores of the six lists.

Company Name	People Rank Score 3x	5 Year Sales Growth Score 2x	5 Year Return on Capital Score 1x	1 Year Return on Capital Score 1x	$ Rev. per Employ. Rank Score 1x	P/E Score 1x
Apple Inc. (AAPL)	51	10	6	8	12	14
Baidu, Inc. (BIDU)	51	4	3	5	18	58

Google Inc. (GOOG)	9	20	23	24	19	48
Samsung Elect Ltd (F) (SSNLF)	42	36	29	13	22	1
Michael Kors Holdings Limited (KORS)	51	6	1	2	45	59
Novo Nordisk A/S (NVO)	63	46	5	1	11	42
Fast Retailing (FRCOY)	33	50	20	19	1	57
Netflix (NFLX)	15	22	14	61	14	71
Coach, Inc. (COH)	63	60	2	3	57	17
Facebook, Inc. (FB)	6	8	57	58	17	71
Cisco Systems, Inc. (CSCO)	18	100	34	31	27	8
Amazon.com Inc. (AMZN)	12	14	31	69	24	69
America Movil (AMX)	132	26	24	41	6	6
ExxonMobile	96	110	10	18	4	4

(XOM)						
Taiwan Semiconductor (TSM)	132	66	12	11	3	19
Costoco Wholesale (COST)	30	76	39	29	30	45
Fomento Economico Mexicano (FMX)	63	58	38	48	10	38
Priceline.com (PCLN)	132	18	7	10	28	60
EOG Resources (EOG)	63	24	47	54	5	65
Potash Corp. (POT)	132	72	13	23	15	9
Oracle Corporation (ORCL)	96	52	27	21	54	18
Gilead Sciences, Inc. (GILD)	132	28	8	26	13	62
JP Morgan Chase (JPM)	3	90	67	59	44	7
Starbucks Corporation	33	78	18	9	73	61

(SBUX)						
Berkshire Hathaway (BRK.A)	27	88	56	52	29	22
BlackRock (BLK)	87	40	52	47	20	30
Tesla Mortors, Inc. (TSLA)	21	2	75	75	38	68
Monsanto Company (MON)	63	96	30	22	32	41
Express Scripts (ESRX)	132	12	28	57	9	53
Wynn Resorts (WYNN)	33	42	64	55	51	56
Abbott Laboratories (ABT)	93	68	32	42	39	33
Anheuser-Busch InBev (BUD)	96	44	61	34	62	13
Intel (INTC)	132	80	22	25	36	15
Yum! Brands (YUM)	63	94	11	15	76	51
TJX (TJX)	132	82	4	4	72	27
IBM (IBM)	96	132	9	7	67	11

Company						
EMC (EMC)	111	54	45	40	46	29
SAP (SAP.AG)	132	64	15	12	65	44
BHP Billiton (BHP)	111	122	19	39	16	26
Yahoo! Inc. (YHOO)	51	148	37	6	41	50
Deere & Co. (DE)	132	70	55	49	31	3
Perrigo (PRGO)	132	38	40	37	47	52
ARM Holdings (ARMH)	111	30	42	36	64	67
Canon (CAJ)	96	146	46	45	2	16
McDonald's (MCD)	111	106	21	17	74	24
Swatch Group (SWGAY)	132	84	26	16	61	36
Ryanair Holdings (RYAAY)	132	48	58	50	34	35
Tesco (TESO)	63	108	54	44	66	23
Group Danone (DANOY)	132	56	44	27	68	34
Enbridge (ENB)	132	32	60	66	8	64
Allergan Inc. (AGN)	132	74	43	35	33	54

Company						
Simon Property Group Inc. (SPG)	63	92	69	65	21	63
Expeditors Int'l (EXPD)	132	118	16	20	40	49
TD Bank Group (TD)	111	62	71	63	56	12
Nordstrom (JWN)	132	86	41	28	69	20
General Electric (GE)	42	140	68	64	37	31
Ford Motor Company (F)	96	144	59	60	23	5
Precision Castparts (PCP)	132	102	25	32	55	43
Sherwin-Williams (SHW)	132	112	17	14	59	55
Tenaris (TS)	132	130	33	33	42	25
ArcelorMittal (MT)	42	142	66	74	53	21
FedEx (FDX)	87	114	49	46	60	47
Procter & Gamble (PG)	132	134	36	38	26	37
Salesforce.com (CRM)	132	16	65	73	48	74
Petrobras	132	138	62	68	7	2

(PZE)						
BYD (BYD)	132	34	50	67	63	70
Honeywell (HON)	132	124	35	30	58	39
Royal Bank of Canada (RY)	132	104	72	62	49	10
American Express (AXP)	132	120	63	56	35	32
CBS (CBS)	132	136	73	43	25	40
Siemens (SI)	126	128	48	51	70	28
SABMiller (SBMRY)	132	126	51	53	52	46
SolarCity Corporation (SCTY)	21	152	76	76	75	75
Dish Network (DISH)	132	98	70	70	43	66
Hewlett Packard (HPQ)	126	116	53	72	50	76
Royal Bank of Scotland (RBS)	132	150	74	71	71	73

Company Name	Total Score	Total Score Ranking
Apple Inc. (AAPL)	101	1
Baidu, Inc. (BIDU)	139	2
Google Inc. (GOOG)	143	3
Samsung Elect Ltd (F) (SSNLF)	143	3
Michael Kors Holdings Limited (KORS)	164	5
Novo Nordisk A/S (NVO)	168	6
Fast Retailing (FRCOY)	180	7
Netflix (NFLX)	197	8
Coach, Inc. (COH)	202	9
Facebook, Inc. (FB)	217	10
Cisco Systems, Inc. (CSCO)	218	11
Amazon.com Inc. (AMZN)	219	12
America Movil (AMX)	235	13
ExxonMobile (XOM)	242	14

Taiwan Semiconductor (TSM)	243	15
Costoco Wholesale (COST)	249	16
Fomento Economico Mexicano (FMX)	255	17
Priceline.com (PCLN)	255	17
EOG Resources (EOG)	258	19
Potash Corp. (POT)	264	20
Oracle Corporation (ORCL)	268	21
Gilead Sciences, Inc. (GILD)	269	22
JP Morgan Chase (JPM)	270	23
Starbucks Corporation (SBUX)	272	24
Berkshire Hathaway (BRK.A)	274	25
BlackRock (BLK)	276	26
Tesla Mortors, Inc. (TSLA)	279	27
Monsanto Company (MON)	284	28

Company		
Express Scripts (ESRX)	291	29
Wynn Resorts (WYNN)	301	30
Abbott Laboratories (ABT)	307	31
Anheuser-Busch InBev (BUD)	310	32
Intel (INTC)	310	32
Yum! Brands (YUM)	310	32
TJX (TJX)	321	35
IBM (IBM)	322	36
EMC (EMC)	325	37
SAP (SAP.AG)	332	38
BHP Billiton (BHP)	333	39
Yahoo! Inc. (YHOO)	333	39
Deere & Co. (DE)	340	41
Perrigo (PRGO)	346	42
ARM Holdings (ARMH)	350	43
Canon (CAJ)	351	44
McDonald's (MCD)	353	45
Swatch Group (SWGAY)	355	46
Ryanair Holdings (RYAAY)	357	47
Tesco (TESO)	358	48

Group Danone (DANOY)	361	49
Enbridge (ENB)	362	50
Allergan Inc. (AGN)	371	51
Simon Property Group Inc. (SPG)	373	52
Expeditors Int'l (EXPD)	375	53
TD Bank Group (TD)	375	54
Nordstrom (JWN)	376	55
General Electric (GE)	382	56
Ford Motor Company (F)	387	57
Precision Castparts (PCP)	389	58
Sherwin-Williams (SHW)	389	59
Tenaris (TS)	395	60
ArcelorMittal (MT)	398	61
FedEx (FDX)	403	62
Procter & Gamble (PG)	403	63
Salesforce.com (CRM)	408	64
Petrobras (PZE)	409	65
BYD (BYD)	416	66
Honeywell (HON)	418	67

Royal Bank of Canada (RY)	429	68
American Express (AXP)	438	69
CBS (CBS)	449	70
Siemens (SI)	451	71
SABMiller (SBMRY)	460	72
SolarCity Corporation (SCTY)	475	73
Dish Network (DISH)	479	74
Hewlett Packard (HPQ)	493	75
Royal Bank of Scotland (RBS)	571	76

I recommend that you purchased the top ranked stocks for your portfolio. Concentrated investment method is better than a diversified portfolio. For Steward Horejsi, he only needs one stock to become a billionaire. If you understand one particular company or key person well, you have certain advantages over other. You understand the company's advantages, and its competition. You can pick this company even if its overall ranking is much lower.

"Do your work, then step back. The only path to serenity. Giving birth and nourishing, having without possessing, acting with no expectations, leading and not trying to control: this is the supreme virtue." -- Lao-tzu's Tao Te Ching

Chapter 6   Patience and Long Term Prospective

"Our favorite holding period is forever." -- Warren Buffett

"In the pursuit of knowledge, every day something is added.

In the practice of the Way, every day something is dropped.

Less and less do you need to force things, until finally you arrive at non-action.

When nothing is done, nothing is left undone.

True mastery can be gained, by letting things go their way.

It can't be gained by interfering." -- Lao-tzu's Tao Te Ching

After deciding what stocks to buy, you may want to know when to sell. As Buffett says their favorite holding period is forever. By the law of compounding interest, your investment will be double in three years if you can earn a 30 percent return per year. If you can hold a stock for 30 years, and the stock average 30% return a year, you will increase your investment more than 2,500 times. Berkshire stock has been earning a 30% return a year for more than 30 years.

You will double your money in 3 years if you earn 30 percent return per year. Money will double in four years if you earn 20 percent return per year; and in eight years if the return is 10 percent. It pays to have a long term prospective. Your long-term capital gain taxes are lower than short term trading gains. Stewart Horejsi became a billionaire by just holding and adding Berkshire Hathaway stocks since 1980.

You should continue hold your investment unless fundamental changes occurred, such as the key person left, died. Other sale situations are return on capital is no longer desirable; sales growth decreased substantially while overall economy is good; or the P/E is becoming unreasonably high. You can sell your investment if you find a better alternative.

If Stewart Horejsi, who became a billionaire by holding Berkshire stocks, holds his stock over 120 years, the stock will increase 50 trillion times in theory if Buffett lived and worked that long. Stewart Horejsi would become a zillionaire. As a lottery TV commercial said, "If you keep on living, we keep paying". I will discuss more on longevity in Chapter 10.

I will discuss some wonderful findings on healthy living in the next few chapters.

"We don't get paid for being busy; we get paid for being right." -- Warren Buffett

PART TWO - Health

Chapter 7   an Ancient Secret Recipe on Dieting

Mr. Ping: The secret ingredient is... nothing!

Po: Huh?

Mr. Ping: You heard me. Nothing! There is no secret ingredient.

Po: Wait, wait... it's just plain old noodle soup? You don't add some kind of special sauce or something?

Mr. Ping: Don't have to. To make something special you just have to believe it's special.

[Po looks at the scroll again, and sees his reflection in it]

Po: There is no secret ingredient... – Kung Fu Panda

Two Meals a Day / Skipping Diner

After graduation from Business School, I have been trying to lose some weight for about ten years without any success. I studied Buddhism in 2011 through the encouragement of a friend on my Chinese blog on NetEase.com. I did learn a lot about the philosophy and daily living of this ancient practice of no foods after noon. However, I thought that the Buddhism's practice of no foods after noon was too extreme. On July 12, 2012, one of Chinese NetEase.com Blog friends posted a great article "Skip Dinner to Cure Hundreds of illnesses". In this article, it cited some interview Q&As by Professor Chengkui Wan, Chief Health and Nutritionist of China's Department of Health. CCTV, the most influential and best-known TV network in China, broadcasted the interview. The article also includes related health and nutritional information about the background and benefits of skipping dinner.

Both Buddhism and Chinese Traditional Medicine (CTM) recommend that no meal and no food after noon. Here noon stands from 11 am to 1 pm. No food after noon is not to save foods or to lose weight but to keep your own body healthy and mind clear. In ancient China, people normally did not eat dinners. People considered eating dinner an immoral behavior. Man who ate dinner would be thought unfit to take the prestigious governmental official entrance exams, and might lose the chance to find a wife. Nowadays, Chinese are used to eat dinner and even another meal after dinner. Extra food intake is not good news.

With no meals after noon, people will not feel the typical slump after dinner. Adults will have more time for leisure, study, or even do some work because he or she no longer needs to prepare the dinner, eat the dinner, and cleanup afterwards. In addition to improve your health, skipping dinner will put more money in your wallet if you do it every day. You can use the money saved to buy vitamins and supplements I will discuss later.

In ancient China, from farmers to emperor, nobody ate dinners. The only dinner people ate was the New York Eve dinner during every Chinese New Year.

In 1949 at the beginning of People's Republic of China, Soviet Union experts criticized Chinese's no dinner custom as unscientific and bad nutritional habits. Those experts wanted China to adopt a three-meal habit. At that time, Soviet Union experts' advices were as holy and unarguable. Most people in the cities started eating dinners, but rural farmers and their families continued the no dinner tradition.

In 1959, modeling after Soviet Union, China set up People's Communes all over the country with free three meals a day. Farmers and their families started eating dinners because the dinners were free. Good time only lasted one year before famines started. Part of the reasons was that everybody could receive the same rewards no matter how much you produced. Gradually people lost their incentives to work hard, food productions decreased.

Western world has a similar saying: "Eat breakfast by yourself, share your lunch with a friend and give your dinner to your enemy".

In 1934, Mary Crowell and Clive McCay of Cornell University discovered that reducing the amount of calories fed to rodents while maintaining micronutrient levels (vitamins and minerals) nearly doubled their life spans. The life extension varied for each species, but on average there was a 30-40% increase in lifespan in both mice and rats (Calorie restriction, 2013). Roy Walford, M.D. and his student Richard Weindruch of UCLA explored these findings in detail by a series of experiments with mice. In 1986, laboratory mice, when fed a diet that restricted their caloric intake by 50% yet maintained nutritional requirements, almost doubled their expected life. The calorie-restricted mice had youthful appearances, longer activity levels, and showed delays in age-related diseases (Walford & Weindruch, 1988).

Reasons for Recommending Skipping Dinners or Two Meals A Day:

(1) Body metabolism is the set of chemical reactions that happen in the cells of our bodies to sustain life. These processes allow people to grow and reproduce, maintain their structures, and respond to their environments. Metabolism is usually divided into two categories. Catabolism breaks down organic matter, for example to harvest energy in cellular respiration. Anabolism uses energy to build components of cells such as proteins and nucleic acids. Human metabolism starts to accelerate around 4 am, and reaches the peak around 4 pm, then starts to decline. We need breakfast and lunch to provide energy for metabolism. If a meal with excessive carbohydrates is consumed, after digestion the excess glucose from breakdown

carbohydrates is first converted into a storage carbohydrate called glycogen. Glycogen is stored in skeletal muscles and liver cells. In muscles it serves as a ready store of energy for muscle contractions. In liver cells glycogen can be readily reconverted into glucose and used in periods of fasting (during sleep or between meals to offer and sustain energy). If there is excessive glucose in the body and the muscle and liver tissues have made its maximal amount of glycogen, the excess glucose is converted to fat.

(2) The average American diet without skipping dinner has excessive carbohydrates, proteins, and fats. That is why people become over weight and become obese. The average American consumes 150 grams of proteins a day, five times the protein our bodies need (Fuhrman MD, 1995). Dinner usually is the largest meal of the day. Dinner usually has more animal meats than breakfast or lunch. The extra amount of protein is very damaging. The breakdown of protein metabolism produces about 15 toxins, which includes urea. These toxins enter our bloodstream and can cause mental confusion and headaches (Fuhrman MD, 1995). If individuals consume protein in excess of their caloric and protein needs, the extra protein will not be stored as protein in your body. Unfortunately such extra protein is converted to and stored as fat. Fat intake in excess of normal body need will be stored as fat in your body.

(3) The human body biological clock works with the sunrise and sunset. Organs work hard during the day, especially your liver, stomach, and intestines. The foods you take require many organs and enzymes to digest complex carbohydrates into sugars, proteins into amino acids. Digesting foods divert your blood supply from your brain, heart, and other organs. Without eating food after noon, your liver, stomach, and pancreas, gallbladder, and intestines get rest. Some people think that sleeping is a waste of time. Sleep provides your body period of rest to repair structural and DNA damages. During the day, your body sometimes is overwhelmed with other daily activities and toxins in your body. The period of fast between today's lunch and tomorrow's breakfast provides your digestive more chance to rest

and repair. If you eat dinner, especially a big dinner very close to sleep, your digestive system will be hard working even during your sleep.

(4) Mitochondria inside your cell are your body's power plant transfer energy from food to adenosine triphosphate (ATP). ATP is the energy your body can use. Think this process of breaking down foods to glucose and ATP as refining gasoline from crude oil. Similar to oil refinery, breaking down and transferring energy produce harmful toxins – free radicals. The free radicals can damage healthy cell, and DNA. Unrepaired DNA can lead to cancer. Body can handle certain amount of free radicals. But, the more foods you eat, the more free radicals the mitochondria produce. Restricted calorie intakes reduce the free radicals produced, thus retard your aging process. Skipping dinners not only reduce the amount of free radicals, but also the frequency of free radicals made. During the fasting period from your last lunch to the next breakfast, your body has more resources and time to repair any DNA and cellular damages.

After reading the article on July 13, 2012, I thought that skipping dinner could work for me and have benefits to my health. I did some research on skipping meal and fasting. On July 20, 2012, I started my skipping dinner practice and kept simple daily records. In one month, I lost 10 pounds, and lost one inch of my waist. In July, my family and I took one-week trip to Disney World in Orlando, Florida. I took a different airline because I got a free round trip from my airline mileages.

My old loose fit jean almost fell without a belt at the security checkpoint of Orlando Airport. Something unexpected happened. The Home Land Security Officer asked me to raise my both hands before entering the whole body scan machine. I couldn't raise my both hands because my belt was in the X-ray machine as required. At that moment I realized that I had lost so much weight and maybe a couple of inches of my waist, so the jean was getting really loose. I raised my hand with a strange pose. My wife was laughing out loud when I told her this episode. On September 20, 2012, I had lost 20 pounds. It is a big accomplishment for me. I have been trying many ways to lose weights for years without any success.

In the Western societies, dinner is usually the name of the main meal of the day. Originally, though, dinner referred to the first meal of the day, eaten around noon, and is still occasionally used for a noontime meal, if it is a large or main meal (Dinner, 2013). Breakfast is an interesting word too. Breakfast stands for breaking your fast (Breakfast, 2013). Skipping your dinner is a good daily fasting for about 18 hours from your last lunch to the next breakfast. Normally without skipping dinner, people have no foods for about 12 hours for overnight. Skipping a meal is not that hard as you think. No dinner can become a daily habit. A day without dinner just resembles any another usual day.

Sometimes the best meal for your health is not having one.

"I don't often meet people who want to suffer cardiovascular disease or whatever, and we get those things as a result of the lifelong accumulation of various types of molecular and cellular damage." -- Aubrey de Grey

Chapter 8   Food Nutrition

"You can live long enough to live forever. Immortality is within our grasp. The knowledge exists, if aggressively applied, for you to slow aging and disease processes to such a degree that you can be in good health and good spirits when the more radical life-extending and life-enhancing technologies become available over the next couple of decades." Ray Kurzweil

All foods contain calories. Foods have two kinds of attributes: energy and nutrients. If foods only give your body energy but no nutrients, these foods are called empty calorie foods. Table sugar and alcohol in beer, wine, and spirits are examples of empty calorie foods. It is not that these foods have no calories, just only calories.

Foods provide two groups of nutrients: (1) macronutrients are carbohydrates, proteins, fats (lipids), and water; and (2) micronutrients are vitamins and minerals.

1.   Energy

Carbohydrates, proteins, and Fat all have calories. 1 gram of carbohydrates provides 4 calories; 1 gram of protein provides 4 calories; and 1 gram of fat provides 9 calories. One pound of body fat provides 3,500 calories. Put it a different way, if you fast one day and half without food, only drinking water, you will lose about one pound of fat. Ideally you want get 2/3 of your diets from carbohydrates, 1/3 from protein and fat. Try to avoid empty calories foods, such as soda.

Losing weight in concept is simple: if the calorie intake is less than the calorie used, you will lose weight; if you calorie intake is more than you needed, you gain weight. You can either reduce your calorie intake by eating less, or you can burn more calories by exercising. The hard part is how to sustain weight loss or maintain an optimum weight. Nowadays, sometimes a piece of snack bar has more calories than you can burn in one-hour workout. The no dinner / 2 meals a day program can help consistently lose weight or maintain weight. When you incorporate exercises into the no dinner program, you can achieve better health.

Suppose that one adult now consumes 2,500 calories a day. A McDonald's thousand plus calories lunch and dinner will do get you that much calories. But, if you start skip diner tomorrow without changing your routine breakfasts and lunches, you can cut about 1,200 calories from your diet. In three days you will cut 3,600 calories, or you will lose one pound of body fat. In one month, you will lose 10 pounds. If you can keep for two months, you can lose 20 pounds. You want to lose weights gradually over time.

In the past, I started to get nervous if my lunch or dinner was late for a couple of hours. I snacked myself to bridge my late meals. When I first started skipping diner, I was nervous. Now I have realized hungry feeling is a more mental thing than a real physical need. So to keep myself calm, for the week of skipping dinner, I drank Powerade Zero. Before skipping dinner, I used to have a couple of snacks after dinner. With no dinner practice, I not only skipped dinner, but also avoided my snacks. After three days, I could skip dinners and drank only water with no snacks following lunches. After one month of no dinners, a two-meal day comes more natural to me. When I was tired, stressed, or upset, I had a stronger urge for a dinner, even a big one. With a short rest after commuting home, the urge usually went away.

2. Macronutrients – Carbohydrates, Proteins, Fats, and Water

Nutrients are chemical substances our body uses to build, maintain, repair tissues, and regulate body processes (Nutrient, 2013). The daily requirements for macronutrients usually exceed 1 gram. The daily requirements for micronutrients are less than 1 gram, usually much smaller. Our digestive system breakdowns complex organic matters to simple ones: carbohydrates to simple sugars (e.g. glucose), proteins to amino acids, and fats to fatty acids and glycerol. When your body has more glucose than its daily work, the excess glucose is converted to glycogen as stored energy. The glycogens are stored in your liver and muscle cells up to 400 grams (14 ounces). Your body converts the extra glucose to fat. The extra fat adds to your hips and belly (Rinzler, 2011).

When you first skip your dinner, your body will start to use the glycogen stored in your liver and muscle cells. If you continue to skip dinner on a daily basis, then your body will start to utilize the fat stored in the fat cells on your hips and bellies. You will gradually losing weight.

The body of a healthy lean man contains about 62 percent water, 16 percent protein, 16 percent fat, 6 percent minerals and vitamins, and less than 1 percent carbohydrate (human nutrition, 2013).

Carbohydrates

You want to consume more complex carbohydrates, such as whole grains, whole oats, and sweet potatoes, and should try to avoid simple carbohydrates, such as sugar. It is better to avoid refined flours, refined wheat, and refined sugar. Refined flours and refined wheat have lost most of its nutrients. Artificially enriched flours do not have many nutrients either. As a general rule, you want to eat live foods that rot or sprout, such as seeds, vegetables, and roots (Maccaro, 2005). We get our carbohydrates from plant foods, such as grains, vegetables, and fruits. Milk and milk products have carbohydrate lactose (sugar); however meat, fish, and poultry contain no carbohydrates. Our bodies use carbohydrates primarily for its glucose for our body's daily energy usage.

Human body cannot make carbohydrates. By photosynthesis green plants convert solar energy into chemical energy, which produces food, wood and the biomass from which fossil fuels are derived (Solar energy, 2013). Chemical energy is stored in the carbohydrate bonds (Chemical energy, 2013). Plants form carbohydrates from carbon dioxide (CO_2) and water (H_2O) to carbohydrates (sugars). The most important job of carbohydrate is to provide your body with energy. Carbohydrates are our bodies' preferred energy sources. Carbohydrates also regulate sugar amount in the blood, provide nutrients for friendly bacteria in intestinal tract, and help absorption of calcium (Rinzler, 2011).

Some weight loss programs suggest that high protein diet with low or no carbohydrates. The theory is that the proteins you take will become muscles, which primarily are water and proteins. They believe that proteins are unlike carbohydrates that excess glucoses become fat on the hips and bellies. Excess proteins (amino acids) are converted to glucose and then to fat, which ends up on your hips and bellies. Additionally, digesting excessive proteins produces many toxins, especially digesting animal origin proteins (Protein nutrient, 2013).

Proteins

Proteins' building blocks are amino acids. To make all the proteins that our bodies need, we need 22 different amino acids. For adults, eight amino acids are essential, which means that our bodies cannot synthesize them and must obtain from food. The eight are isoleucine, leucine, lysine, methionine, phenylalanine, threonine, tryptophan, and valine. For children, arginine and histidine are two additional essential amino acids (Rinzler, 2011).

The common American diet has more proteins from foods of animal origin – meat, fish, poultry, eggs, and dairy products than from foods of plant origin. Soybeans have sufficient amounts of all the amino acids essential to human health.

Fats (Lipids)

Polyunsaturated liquid fats are called oils; solid fats are called fat. Saturated and monounsaturated fats are non-essential nutrients, which means that you do not need them. Polyunsaturated fats (oils) are essential nutrients (Rinzler, 2011).

Your body needs fats. The brain is made of 60 percent fat (Nourish - Fats, 2013). In the Western diet, most people eat too much saturated fat, the bad fats, and too little of the essential fats, the good fats. Most people are deficient in two essential fats: omega-3 and omega-6 fats. You can get omega-3 from flax, hemp, and pumpkin seeds. You can get omega-3 fats EPA and DHA in mackerel, lake trout, salmon, tuna, sardines, swordfish, and white fish (Rinzler, 2011).

King's Breakfast and Prince's Lunch

When you skip dinners, it is important that you eat good breakfasts. A nutritional breakfast will include whole oats, soymilk, an apple, and if possible an egg. You need a full lunch. A full meal means about 70% felt full, because the complex carbohydrates take time to be digested to signal the fullness to your brain.

3. Micronutrients - Vitamins and Minerals

A lot of people think that vitamins and minerals are optional. This is a wrong concept. Without sufficient vitamins and minerals you cannot achieve good health. For example, human beings cannot survive without vitamin C after 2 to 3 months; they will die from scurvy. Scurvy is a disease resulting from deficiency of vitamin C. Synthesis of collagen in human requires vitamin C. Vitamin C is also an important antioxidant vitamin involved in the development of connective tissues, lipid and vitamin metabolism, synthesis of neurotransmitters, immune function, and wound healing (Vitamin C, 2013).

Most animals can synthesize their own vitamin C; therefore will not develop scurvy. Human and other higher primates, most bats, and some birds and fishes lack an enzyme (L-gulonolactone oxidase) needed for the synthesis of vitamin C through their foods (Vitamin C, 2013). Plants have vitamin C, with high concentrations in citrus fruits (oranges, lemons, limes, and grapefruits), tomatoes, potatoes, cabbages, and green pepper.

In ancient marine times, ships were found intact but the sailors were all dead from bleeding all over the bodies. It was a mystery for a while. Who or what killed these sailors?

With the discovery of vitamin C, it is known that scurvy is caused by deficiency of vitamin C. The sailors were killed because they did not have had any fresh fruits and vegetables for an extended period. Scurvy is curable and preventable by eating fresh fruits and vegetables, or taking vitamin C supplements. To maintain a good health, Patrick Holford recommends 500 mg a day of vitamin C (Holford, 2005). Dr. Linus Pauling, a twice Nobel Prize Winners, and a Vitamin C advocate, took more than 1,000 mg per day (Vitamin C, 2013). Vitamin C is also a powerful antioxidant.

Cardiovascular Diseases

Cardiovascular diseases, such as heart attacks, strokes (blockages of the brain arteries) are completely preventable. Deposits form in the artery wall, and the deposits are called arterial plaques.

Presence of arterial deposits is called atherosclerosis (Atherosclerosis, 2013). Atherosclerosis can lead to blockage in an artery, thus stops the blood flow. Blockage occurs in the arteries feeding the heart leads to heart attack. Blockage happens in the brain leads a stroke. Why does formation of deposit happen? Free radicals and toxins in the body can damage the lining of arteries. If your body has sufficient vitamin C, your body can use vitamin C to make collagen and to repair the damages.

According to Dr. Linus Pauling and Dr. Matthias Rath, a cardiologist, during vitamin C deficiency periods, our body will deposit lipoproteins along the artery wall to temporary repair damaged or leaky blood vessels. Two types of proteins are normally accumulated at the injury sites for repairs are fibrinogen and lipoprotein A (LpA). LpA is very sticky, which cause continued buildup of artery plagues. The repair performed by vitamin C leave the artery wall smooth and stronger. If vitamin C is available, body will unlikely to use LpA for artery repairs. Although LpA has an important function in the body, Matthias Rath, M.D., considers LpA 10 times more dangerous than LDL cholesterol (Pauling & Rath, 1990).

Laboratory mice, when fed a diet that restricted their caloric intake by 50% yet maintained nutritional requirements, doubled their expected life. To increase life expectancy by restricting calorie intake is conditioned on maintaining nutritional requirements. We can reduce our calorie intake from macronutrients (carbohydrates, proteins, and fats), but we must provide our bodies with sufficient micronutrients (vitamins and minerals).

Occasional fasting is a good body detoxification (detox for short) method if done correctly (Detoxification, 2013). Some fasting programs recommend fasting with only water. I do not agree this method because our bodies still need vitamins and minerals to function properly. Especially, our body does not store water-soluble vitamins, such as vitamin C.

Other Vitamins

Vitamins are organic chemicals, which occurs naturally in all living things in both plants and animals. For optimum health, our body needs at least 11 vitamins: vitamin A, vitamin D, vitamin E, vitamin K, vitamin C, and the members of the B vitamin family – thiamin (vitamin B1), riboflavin (B2), niacin, vitamin B6, folic acid, and vitamin B12 (Rinzler, 2011).

Fat-soluble Vitamins

Vitamin A, vitamin D, vitamin E, and vitamin K are all fat-soluble. They are stored in our fatty tissues (Vitamin, 2013).

Scientists found that a healthy person produce some cancerous cells in his or her body. Because our immune system, these cancer cells are killed and cause no harm to our body. Cancer cells are normal body cells are out of control. Normal cells will die within certain period. Cancer cells will not die and will reproduce themselves indefinitely. The cancer cells take nutrients from normal body cells.

We should eat balanced diets with macronutrients and micronutrients, preferably organic foods (Organic food, 2013) and whole foods (Whole food, 2013), not processed foods. In addition, we should exercise regularly, keep positive attitudes, and sleep well, to achieve a long and healthy life.

US Department of Agriculture's MyPlate nutrition guide is divided into sections of approximately 30 percent grains, 30 percent vegetables, 20 percent fruits and 20 percent protein, accompanied by a smaller circle representing dairy, such as a glass of low-fat/nonfat milk or a yogurt cup (MyPlate, 2013).

The U.S. Food and Drug Administration recommended the following table listing the Daily Values based on a caloric intake of 2,000 calories, for adults and children four or more years of age (Guidance for Industry: A Food Labeling Guide (14. Appendix F: Calculate the Percent Daily Value for the Appropriate Nutrients), 2013).

Food Component	Daily Value
Total Fat	65 grams (g)
Saturated Fat	20 g

Cholesterol	300 milligrams (mg)
Sodium	2,400 mg
Potassium	3,500 mg
Total Carbohydrate	300 g
Dietary Fiber	25 g
Protein	50 g
Vitamin A	5,000 International Units (IU)
Vitamin C	60 mg
Calcium	1,000 mg
Iron	18 mg
Vitamin D	400 IU
Vitamin E	30 IU
Vitamin K	80 micrograms μg
Thiamin	1.5 mg
Riboflavin	1.7 mg
Niacin	20 mg
Vitamin B6	2 mg
Folate	400 μg
Vitamin B12	6 μg
Biotin	300 μg
Pantothenic acid	10 mg
Phosphorus	1,000 mg
Iodine	150 μg
Magnesium	400 mg
Zinc	15 mg
Selenium	70 μg

Copper	2 mg
Manganese	2 mg
Chromium	120 μg
Molybdenum	75 μg
Chloride	3,400 mg

Chapter 9   Eczema, Asthma, Sleeping Disorders, and Joint Pains

"By preventing 90 percent of medical problems, life expectancy grows to over five hundred years. At 99 percent, we'd be over one thousand years. We can expect that the full realization of the biotechnology and nanotechnology revolutions will enable us to eliminate virtually all-medical causes of death. As we move toward a nonbiological existence, we will gain the means of 'backing ourselves up' (storing the key patterns underlying our knowledge, skills, and personality), thereby eliminating most causes of death as we know it." -- Ray Kurzweil

In 2006, a few months after our first daughter Marilyn was born in New York, we sent her to live with my parents in Kunming, China. My parents hired a live in nanny for Marilyn. Marilyn developed severe eczema problems.

Doctors prescribed 2 percent hydrocortisone cream for Marilyn's eczema both in the US and in China. People usually have misunderstandings and fears about hormone medications. Cortisone is a steroid hormone. My wife was against using the cortisone. Her reason was that cortisone was bad for Marilyn's skin. Then both my mother and my sister in China were also against using cortisone cream for the same reason. I have allergies to dust mites, cockroaches, and a few pollens. My wife did not want to get tested for allergy. She did not think that she had any allergies.

Allergies are the overreaction of our immune system to normally harmless substances. The substances are called allergens. My allergens are dust mites, cockroaches, and certain pollens. Cortisone's primary functions are to increase blood sugar through gluconeogenesis; suppress the immune system; and aid in fat, protein and carbohydrate metabolism (Cortisone, 2013).

Cortisone down regulates the interleukin-2, a signal molecule of the immune system. My Master's degree thesis was on the relationships between several interleukins and heat shock proteins. Down regulated interleukin-2 results in less B cells antibody production. An antibody is a large Y-shaped protein produced by B cells that is used by the immune system to identify and neutralize foreign objects such as bacteria, viruses, and allergens. Cortisone prevents the release of substances in the body that cause inflammation. This is why cortisone is used to treat conditions resulting from over-activity of the B-cell antibody response such as inflammatory and rheumatoid diseases, and allergies. Low-potency cortisone, or hydrocortisone, is used to treat skin problems such as rashes, eczema and others. One side effect scientists found is loss of collagens of lab animals treated with cortisone.

    My daughter Marilyn later developed allergy-induced asthma since she was two in China. She was hospitalized a few times for asthma related illness. I told my mom and my sister, who is a nurse to get allergy tests for Marilyn. They told me that allergy skin or blood tests were not available in Kunming, although a large city in China. One day after midnight, my sister called me from China. She told me that a hospital told them Marilyn was in critical condition because her asthma induced illnesses. We were shocked and really worried. Luckily Marilyn got through that winter.

    I took Marilyn back to the US when she was four. Her face was all messed up because of eczema. I took her to an allergist for allergy skin tests. The tests confirmed that Marilyn had severe allergies to most meat, all nuts, egg whites, egg yolk, soy, beans, many pollens, and dust mites. The only two kinds of meats she could eat were fish and lamb. The doctor put Marilyn on weekly allergy shot, or immunotherapy.

    The allergy shots are used to desensitizing your immune system for allergens. Each allergy shot contains a tiny amount of allergens. Allergy shots contain enough allergens to stimulate the immune system, but not enough to trigger full-blown allergic reactions. Over time, doctors increase the dose of the allergens.

Your body builds up tolerance of allergens, and allergy symptoms diminish over time.

It is common that children with allergic eczema will also have asthma. Asthma is usually caused by allergic inflammation of the respiratory airways. After a couple months of allergy shots coupling with avoidance of allergic foods, to our relief, Marilyn's health improved greatly. Rashes used to be all over her face cleared up too.

The name allergy or immune system over-sensitive is kind misleading. Allergy is caused by somewhat malfunction of the immune system. In her first grade, Marilyn missed a few classes due to sickness and failing to go to field trips because of motion sickness. I ordered my daughters daily children's multi-vitamins and children immune support supplements. Now Marilyn is beautiful, healthy 3rd grade honor student. She has also outgrown her food allergies.

My wife later had allergy test done. She has allergies to dust mites, cockroaches, some foods, and many types of pollens. Our 2nd daughter Michelle was born in 2009; and our son, Michael was born in 2009. Both of them have allergies, but none of them suffered what Marilyn went through. We gave them prescribed cortisone creams as soon as eczema symptoms developed. 1 percent cortisone creams are available over the counter in drug stores in the U.S.

Back in China, my mom's friends were still worrying about Marilyn's rashes over her faces. My mom told them several times that Marilyn had no skin problems any more. I told my mom it was because of the allergy tests and allergy shots. I am not sure my mom understood what that means. Her friends still do not understand what happened, because in Kunming, there are still no allergy shots available according to my nurse sister. They would say, "The medical technologies in the US are much better than those in China".

Cortisone is hormone that its functions are still to be fully understood. Questcor Pharmaceuticals, Inc. (QCOR) has a market capitalization over $3 billion. Its main product is H.P. Acthar Gel for the treatment of multiple sclerosis, nephritic syndrome, and infant spasms. Acthar's principal effects are increased production and release of cortisone. Aventis developed Acthar in the 1950s. In 2001, Questcor bought Acthar from Aventis for $100,000 plus 1 percent royalty on annual sales over $10 million. Questcor successfully increased the unit price of a 5-milliliter vial from $50 to $28,000 over the years (Pollack, 2012). In 2012, sales of Acthar, which accounted for essentially all of Questcor's sales, totaled more than $620 million (Press Releases, 2013).

Sleeping Disorders

I had occasional insomnia for a while. I tried listening to soft ocean sounds before sleeping. It did not work for me. I tried Ambien, Ambien CR. Ambien worked, but it was habit forming. I stopped taking Ambien after a while.

One day, I was reading an article on Shi Yuzhu. He was once the richest person in 1990s in China. He went into bankruptcy after trying to build the highest building in China at that time. However he successfully turned himself around by one product – Brian Platinum. The story intrigued me to learn more about Brian Platinum.

The main ingredient of Brain Platinum is melatonin. Melatonin is a natural human hormone produced by the brain's pineal gland. Melatonin regulates the sleep-wake cycle. Human melatonin production decreases as people ages. Besides helping people sleeping better, melatonin also has antioxidant, and anti-aging functions. In the U.S., Melatonin is not regulated by the FDA, but regarded as food a supplement.

I used 3 mg melatonin regularly. It helped my mild insomnia without the side effects of prescription insomnia drugs.

Joint Pains

I started jogging in high school. It has been one of my hobbies. However 15 years ago, after running a Corporate Challenge in Central Park, I had severe pains on my knees. Because my sedative works, I sit most of the time. I also had back and neck problems. I tried physical therapy, acupunctures, and chiropractors. My chiropractor helped my back problems. He recommended me to do stretching before and after jogging, especially after exercises. The stretching helped a little bite.

One day, I was complaining to my family doctor about my knee problem. My doctor said why not to try Nature Made Triple Flex with Glucosamine, Chondroitin, and MSM Caplets. Her patients found good results with this product. She told me that the knees were just like machine parts. The knees have wears and tears. Knees carry weights over a hundred pounds every day. The burden increases when you are running. The soft cartridge wears off year after year. I tried Triple Flex for two weeks. One day, when I was walking up the subway stairs, I felt my knees were so comfortable and fluid. This was a feeling that I had not felt in 20 years. Triple Flex helped my knees.

"By the 2030s, the nonbiological portion of our intelligence will predominate." -- Ray Kurzweil

Chapter 10 Aging is Merely a Curable Disease

"My approach is to start from the straightforward principle that our body is a machine. A very complicated machine, but none the less a machine, and it can be subjected to maintenance and repair in the same way as a simple machine, like a car." -- Aubrey de Grey

"We are in the early stages of multiple profound revolutions spawned by the intersection of biology, information science, and nanotechnology. With the decoding of the genome and our effects to decode its expression in proteins, many new and powerful methodologies are emerging. These include rational drug design (drugs designed for every precise missions with little or no side effects), tissue engineering (regrowing our cells, tissues, and organs), reversal of aging processes, gene therapy (essentially reprogramming our genetic code), nanobots (robots the size of blood cells built from molecules placed in our bodies and bloodstreams to enhance every aspect of our lives), and many others." --Ray Kurzweil

Just like mental diseases in earlier times, people usually do not think aging as a disease. Aging is accumulations of damages at different levels. DNA and proteins damages are at molecular level. Cancers occurs at cellular levels. Heart diseases are at organ levels because of lack of maintenance or restoring to their pre-damage conditions (de Grey & Rae, 2008). A human body is like a car or computer. All parts need to function well. There are cars run like new after decades of usages. Buildings last more than a thousand year with proper maintenances. Irv Gordon has well maintained his 1966 Volvo, and has run close to 3 million miles on this car. His 1966 Volvo still runs like new (Stump, 2013).

Recently a team of engineers has created robot using artificial limbs, artificial organs, and other body parts that resemble a "bionic" man (The Incredible Bionic Man, 2013). In a sense human body is like a computer. DNA stores all the software information in genes on the chromosomes. If the DNA software gets damaged, the damages will lead to cancers and many other diseases. Like a computer, a body needs energy from foods to work. Our bodies can only use glucose as energy. All living organisms and most of our energy come from the sun. Plants convert the solar energy to chemical energy in the form of chemical bonds. The energy passes on through the food chains in our ecosystem. Oil and gas are plant and animal fossils buried undergrounds.

Mitochondria inside our cells are the energy power plants. Glucose energy is converted to ATP, the energy cells can use for their functions. One side effect of mitochondrial energy conversion is the production of free radicals. Free radicals are highly reactive, and can cause a lot damages to molecules, cellular structures in our bodies. Antioxidants can neutralize free radicals.

Sleeps are thought to be useful in repair the damages at molecular and cellular levels. Immune system and stem cells are our bodies' defense and repair mechanisms to repair and heal. Stem cells act as the natural renewal system of the body. Human babies have 25 million stem cells. At the age of 65, human adults only have 5 million stem cells left (Increase your Stem Cells Naturally!, 2013). Maintaining healthy number of stem cells is important to our health.

Stem cells are undifferentiated cells that can divide into more stem cells or specialized cells, such as skin cells, or heart cells, etc. In adults, there are three major sources of stem cells in our bodies – bone marrow, lipid cells, and blood (Stem cell, 2013). Cancer patients on radiation treatments sometimes need bone marrow transplants to receive other people's stem cells. Scientists found that blue green algae Aphanizomenon flos-aquae can enhance body's stem cell production (Shytle, et al., 2010). You can purchase blue green algae in health food stores.

Our body cells and tissues sustain damages through our life. Our bodies can tolerate some damages. Extended damages lead to diseases and aging if the damages are not repaired promptly or well repaired. You might have fillings or crowns for your teeth. These are small non-human body parts. People may have artificial knee or hip replacements to replace their canes. People have Lasik surgeries to improve their visions, and hearing aids to improve their hearings. Replacement hearts, lungs, livers, and kidneys are more common surgery procedures in advanced countries. You can see the trend that your body is receiving more and more replacement artificial and biological parts.

Existing experimental and upcoming biotechnologies will greatly improve people's health and increase the longevity. Doctors recommended that you collect and store your newborn children's stem cells. The prices are reasonable. The stem cells can restore your children's health if needed and can prolong their life in the future. In the field of regenerative medicine, scientists can grow almost any artificial human organs in the labs using stem cells or sometimes non-stem cells. Scientists use your own cells to grow the organs, such as a new heart, or a new lung. Because the organs use your own cells, so your body will not reject the heart. The new heart will be just like your old heart only better, unlike organ transplants that you need to take life-long immunosuppressant drugs to prevent organ failures (Naik, 2013).

With the increasing of computing power and shrinking of the size of computer, Ray Kurzweil believes that our lives will be enhanced with advances in nanobots in the near future. Nanobots are micro robots of the size of our blood cells. Nanobots will be placed in our bloodstreams to enhance our bodily functions (Kurzweil, 2006).

Biologist and technologist Aubrey de Grey outlined seven damages rising with age and methods to reverse these damages to end aging:
(1) Cell therapy to treat cell losses and cell atrophy.

(2) Telomerase / ACT gene deletion plus period stem cell reseeding to treat division-obsessed cells (i.e. cancers).
(3) Suicide genes and immune stimulation to treat death-resistant cells.
(4) Allotopic expression of 13 proteins to treat mitochondrial mutations.
(5) Transgenic microbalhdroleases to treat intracellular junk.
(6) Immune stimulated Phagocytosis to treat extracellular junk.
(7) Advanced Glycation End Products – breaking molecules / enzymes to repair extracellular crosslinks (de Grey & Rae, 2008).

Two key factors for aging and longevity are the maintenance of stem cells and the maintenance of a functional immune system. A balanced diet includes carbohydrates, proteins, and lipids, plus sufficient amount of vitamins and minerals. Fruits and vegetables, organic foods, and whole foods are good for you. Regular exercising, having good sleeps, and thinking positively can maintain and improve your immune system.

"We have the means right now to live long enough to live forever. Existing knowledge can be aggressively applied to dramatically slow down aging processes so we can still be in vital health when the more radical life extending therapies from biotechnology and nanotechnology become available. But most baby boomers won't make it because they are unaware of the accelerating aging process in their bodies and the opportunity to intervene." -- Ray Kurzweil

PART THREE - Government, Health Care, Housing, STEM, and Knowledge Economy

Chapter 11 Government: The Party – Which Party?

"It is essential to rear a generation at the very top of society that has all the qualities needed to lead and give the people the inspiration and the drive to make it succeed. In short, the elite…every society tries to produce this type. The British have special schools for them: the gifted and talented are sent to Eton and Harrow." – Lee Kuan Yew, Prime Minister of Singapore, August 1966

When the Tao is lost, there is goodness. When goodness is lost, there is morality. When morality is lost, there is ritual. Ritual is the husk of true faith, the beginning of chaos.
Therefore the Master concerns himself with the depths and not the surface, with the fruit and not the flower. He has no will of his own. He dwells in reality, and lets all illusions go. – Lao Tzu's Tao Te Ching

The two most important reasons that China succeeded in the past 35 years is because China's leaders followed Mao Thought and followed Singapore economic model for openness and reforms. Mao's Thought has been usually misunderstood in China and more misunderstood in the Western societies. As Larry Hsien Ping Lang, a popular TV host in China, and a former Wharton Finance professor, said very few people in the world really understood Mao Thought and its significance of Mao Thought. Deng's most important contribution to China was his Reform and Opening to the World Though. Current Chinese leader Xi Jinping is more or less following Mao Thought. Mao himself said he did not know much about economy and development. The only foreign country Mao visited was the Soviet Union. Mao modeled China's economy after the Soviet Union. Deng traveled to France to work and study when he was 16 and spent 7 years in Europe.

Deng Xiaoping said, "Mao Zedong Thought in the essence is seeking truth from facts". That is daring to seek the truths no matter how unpopular the truths are, and to seek the principles from the truths. Starting by seeking truth, finding rules, and devising solutions; second, you test your solutions. Making improvements; Facing new problems, seeking new truth, and new solutions; Making better improvements. This process repeats until forever. Former Chairman and CEO of DuPont Charles Holliday, Jr. said "A company can operate successfully for 200 years only by continually reinventing itself" (Orloski, 2002). Samsung Electronics succeeds in becoming the largest information technology company by continuous reinventing itself, insisting a sense of perpetual crisis. The crisis mentality works for a company as well as for a country.

Mao's military strategies are studied at Military Academies around the world. Mao's Thought can be also applied to economics and corporate management. Religion and scientific development sometimes have conflicted for over centuries. At times religious believes impeded the development of sciences and economics. There is the separation of the Churches and state, but not enough.

U.S. should be more tolerant for alternative views besides traditional Christianity and Catholics. For example, many states and federal governments have restrictions or even completed ban on stem cell research (Stem cell laws and policy in the United States, 2013). Exploring alternative believes, such as Buddhism, and even atheism, such as Albert Einstein and Steve Jobs did, should be encouraged.

Both of my parents started their career as civil engineers in the same company after graduated from the same college in Yunnan, before the start of Cultural Revolution. My mother's families were from a coastal province, Zhejiang, China. Her father was a bus station manager, but he died during the war when Japan invaded China. My mother's elder uncle was one of the early students to Europe, and a friend of Chinese Premier Zhou En Lai.

Japanese bombs destroyed this uncle's chemical plant in China. My mother's younger uncle was a teacher in Kunming, Yunnan. This uncle later adopted my mother. This was the grandfather I knew. He later became a physics professor in Yunnan University.

My paternal grandfather, Bo Shi, joined Mao's army against the Japanese. He became a Division Commander in the Chinese Army. After leaving the military, he was assigned as the in Deputy Director of Forestry Department of Yunnan Province. My father got a job in old man's Department after college. My grandfather Bo Shi came from a rural village. He taught himself to read and to write. He married my grandmother from a nearby village, when they were young. My grandmother barely knew how to write her own name. They had three sons. My father was their 2nd son. My grandfather later divorced my grandmother. At that time in China, remarriage was rarely tolerated, especially for senior officials. My grandfather was disciplined and demoted after the second marriage. He made a lateral move to Hunan Province, his hometown. He had three more children in the second marriage. His wife and three children worked in the agency where he was in charge. I met my paternal grandfather Bo Shi twice.

China started economic reform in 1978. Since 1950s, Mao encouraged and forced millions of youth ("Zhiqing") in the cities to work in the countryside or rural mountainous regions. Mao closed all colleges in China for ten years during the Cultural Revolution. He wanted them to build the countryside and to learn from the peasants. Mao sent thousands college professors, teachers, office workers, and scientists to the countryside to be reeducated. In 1977, China resumed college educations, and allowed students to take the college entrance exams. Since 1978, Deng tried to get the professors, teachers, and scientists back to the cities.

Starting 1978, millions of Zhiqing youths poured back to the cities. However, China had not enough job opening to absorb these returnees. The government tried to solve the unemployment problems for millions by encouraging these youths or middle aged to become self-employed. That marked the beginning of private enterprises after the Cultural Revolution. In the same time, government started experimenting by dividing People's Commune farmlands, and allowed farmer families to own and manage their own parcels of farmland. Farmers could keep and sell whatever above productions above agreed upon quotas. The experiment for farmers became an instant success. Crop productions increased dramatically. Farmers were happy to get up early and stay late to care for their crops. The renewed enthusiasms had been seen in decades since the start of People's Communes in 1958. Deng Xiaoping's "let some people get rich first" motivated Chinese to work harder and smarter.

To catch up with the United States and the United Kingdom quickly, Mao started People's Communes as part of the Great Leap Forward campaign in rural countryside in 1958. A Commune consisted of 4,000 to 20,000 households. Most personal belongings were shared in a Commune. People contributed their cooking utensils, chairs, tables, and foods to the Commune's kitchen. Private cooking was banned. Other private personal belongings were also contributed to the Commune, such as private animals, and grains. People were supposed to eat all they want in the Commune's kitchens.

Commune's leaders centrally assigned everyone a job. In some places, even money was outlawed. Soon, people started to realize that they would get the same no matter how hard they worked. Food productions decreased. Laziness with bad weather in 1958-1960, famines were widespread. However, the People's Commune structure remained until early 1980s (People's commune, 2013).

Although Mao made mistakes such as the Great Leap Forward, the Cultural Revolution, Mao made significant contribution to the modern China. As an article stated on the New York Times dated September 10, 1976, "Born at a time when China was wracked by civil strife, beset with terrible poverty and encroached on by more advanced foreign powers, he lived to fulfill his boyhood dream of restoring it to its traditional place as a great nation. I n Chinese terms, he ranked with Chin Shih-huang, the first Emperor, who unified China in 221 B.C., and was the man Chairman Mao most liked to compare himself to…Then, after establishing the Chinese People's Republic, Mao launched a series of sweeping, sometimes convulsive campaigns to transform a semi feudal, largely illiterate and predominantly agricultural country encompassing almost four million square miles and a fifth of the world's population into a modern, industrialized socialist state. By the time of his death China had manufactured its own nuclear bombs and guided missiles and had become a major oil producer" (Butterfield, 1976).

After Deng assumed the leadership, he rallied the "Four Modernizations," which called for the development of industry, agriculture, defense, and science and technology. With the dismantlement of the communes, Deng introduced the Household Responsibility System. Each household was held accountable to the state for only what it agreed to produce, and could keep surplus output for private use. In addition to this incentive program, Deng encouraged farmers to engage in private entrepreneurship and sideline businesses to supplement their incomes. As Samsung Chair Lee Kun-hee said "Monetary reward system is a great human invention, which is the determining factor that capitalism triumphed over communism".

Deng Xiaoping stressed, "Practice is the sole criterion of truth." He encouraged the country to be brave and experiment with alternative forms of production and entrepreneurship to find a better path for economic development. China began experiments with capitalist methods of production, or "to cross the river by touching the stones". As Deng said, "it does not matter whether a cat is black or white so long as it catches the mouse". It did not matter whether an economic policy was capitalist or socialist. In other words, it was a good policy as long as it resulted in economic growth.

Another two phrases that Deng usually said was that we all made mistakes, including himself and Mao. Like cleaning our houses often, we should clean my thoughts and ideas often.

Before 1990, all Chinese colleges assigned jobs to college graduates in government agencies, colleges, or government owned companies. The private companies were few and small. Government just started to allow private enterprises in special economic zones. Most of the special economic zones were in Guangdong Province. At the beginning, government allowed individuals or family members to start private business, but could not hire any employees. As these individual businesses grew, successful ones started to hire employees. China debated whether hiring employees was legal under a socialist society, and what would be the maximum employees a private business could hire. After many heated discussions, the government decided that hiring maximum eight employees were legal. Because someone found that Carl Marx defined someone a capitalist if he hired more than eight employees in his book "The Capital".

Soon, private enterprises secretly hired more than eight employees. The discussion then was whether government should jail these capitalists. Some of these capitalists started to write to central government expressing their concerns. Deng said in People's Daily, the central government newspaper, "let some people get rich first" and "to get rich is glorious". Deng cited Nian Guangjiu, whose factory made "Idiot Sunflower Seeds", as an example. This factory hired more than 100 employees (Chinese capitalism The long march backwards, 2008).

Deng toured several southern China provinces and their special economic zones in 1992. After the tour, China Daily published his famous Southern Tour Speech. The Speech praised the rapid economic developments in the special economic zones and encouraged more private enterprises. After the Speech, many government officials left their jobs to become entrepreneurs. College graduates started working for private companies instead of the more prestigious government agencies, or government owned companies. Many China Forbes 400 people started their business after Deng's Southern Tour Speech.

Mao Though "Seek truth from facts" is a summary of his earlier ideas. In his 1937 article "On Contradiction" (On Contradiction, 2013); Mao Tse-tung said, "Lenin meant just this when he said that the most essential thing in Marxism, the living soul of Marxism, is the individual analysis based on particular conditions (Circumstances alter cases). Our dogmatists have violated Lenin's teachings; they never use their brains to analyze anything concretely, and in their writings and speeches they always use stereotypes devoid of content, thereby creating a very bad style of work in our Party" (Mao, 1937).

According to Preamble of Constitution of the People's Republic of China (Adopted on December 4, 1982), "The basic task of the nation in the years to come is to concentrate its effort on socialist modernization. Under the leadership of the Communist Party of China and the guidance of Marxism- Leninism and Mao Zedong Thought, the Chinese people of all nationalities will continue to adhere to the people's democratic dictatorship and follow the socialist road, steadily improve socialist institutions, develop socialist democracy, improve the socialist legal system and work hard and self-reliantly to modernize industry, agriculture, national defense and science and technology step by step to turn China into a socialist country with a high level of culture and democracy" (Contitution of the People's Republic of China, 1982).

"As opposed to the metaphysical world outlook, the world outlook of materialist dialectics holds that in order to understand the development of a thing we should study it internally and in its relations with other things; in other words, the development of things should be seen as their internal and necessary self-movement, while each thing in its movement is interrelated with and interacts on the things around it. The fundamental cause of the development of a thing is not external but internal; it lies in the contradictoriness within the thing. There is internal contradiction in every single thing, hence its motion and development.

Contradictoriness within a thing is the fundamental cause of its development, while its interrelations and interactions with other things are secondary causes. Thus materialist dialectics effectively combats the theory of external causes, or of an external motive force, advanced by metaphysical mechanical materialism and vulgar evolutionism. It is evident that purely external causes can only give rise to mechanical motion, that is, to changes in scale or quantity, but cannot explain why things differ qualitatively in thousands of ways and why one thing changes into another. As a matter of fact, even mechanical motion under external force occurs through the internal contradictoriness of things. Simple growth in plants and animals, their quantitative development, is likewise chiefly the result of their internal contradictions. Similarly, social development is due chiefly not to external but to internal causes. Countries with almost the same geographical and climatic conditions display great diversity and unevenness in their development" (Mao, 1937).

"For convenience of exposition, I shall deal first with the universality of contradiction and then proceed to the particularity of contradiction. The reason is that the universality of contradiction can be explained more briefly, for it has been widely recognized ever since the materialist-dialectical world outlook was discovered and materialist dialectics applied with outstanding success to analyzing many aspects of human history and natural history and to changing many aspects of society and nature (as in the Soviet Union) by the great creators and continuers of Marxism- -Marx, Engels, Lenin and Stalin; whereas the particularity of contradiction is still not dearly understood by many comrades, and especially by the dogmatists. They do not understand that it is precisely in the particularity of contradiction that the universality of contradiction resides. Nor do they understand how important is the study of the particularity of contradiction in the concrete things confronting us for guiding the course of revolutionary practice. Therefore, it is necessary to stress the study of the particularity of contradiction and to explain it at adequate length. For this reason, in our analysis of the law of contradiction in things, we shall first analyze the universality of contradiction, then place special stress on analyzing the particularity of contradiction, and finally return to the universality of contradiction."

"The universality or absoluteness of contradiction has a twofold meaning. One is that contradiction exists in the process of development of all things, and the other is that in the process of development of each thing a movement of opposites exists from beginning to end."

"Engels said, "Motion itself is a contradiction." Lenin defined the law of the unity of opposites as "the recognition (discovery) of the contradictory, mutually exclusive, opposite tendencies in all phenomena and processes of nature (including mind and society)". Are these ideas correct? Yes, they are. The interdependence of the contradictory aspects present in all things and the struggle between these aspects determine the life of all things and push their development forward. There is nothing that does not contain contradiction; without contradiction nothing would exist. Contradiction is the basis of the simple forms of motion (for instance, mechanical motion) and still more so of the complex forms of motion" (Mao, 1937).

After stabilizing the political turmoil in November 1978, Deng Xiaoping visited Prime Minister Lee Kuan Yew, and a hard line anti-communist leader in Singapore. Singapore was a prosperous and rapidly growing country. Since that visit, Deng and Lee had developed special bonds. In Lee's two-part memoirs, The Singapore Story: "I had never met a communist leader who was prepared to depart from his brief when confronted with reality," he wrote, "much less ask what I wanted him to do." Mr. Lee paid tribute to the reformer Deng: "He was the most impressive leader I had met. He was a five-footer, but a giant among men. At 74, when he was faced with an unpleasant truth, he was prepared to change his mind" (Yew, 1998).

Mr. Lee advised Deng to open up China and to reform economically. Deng said to Lee that things would be easier if he were only the mayor of Shanghai, instead of the leader of the whole China. Mr. Lee told Deng that most of the people of his tiny country were descents of immigrants from China a few generations ago. These early generation immigrants were not the elites of China, but the lowly migrant village people who tried to make a living in nearby countries. Lee said that a country's prosperity mainly resulted from good policies towards openness and reforms. Lee challenged Deng that if Singapore could achieve such success, China should be able to do better. Deng went silent. After the visit, China sent tens of thousands of peoples to Singapore to study the Singapore Model. China has primarily followed the Singapore Economic Model. Years later after Deng's Southern Tour Speech published, Lee was amazed to read that Deng was telling senior Chinese leaders to study the Singapore and to do better than Singapore. So Deng never forgot about Lee's challenge to him.

Deng said, "Poverty is not socialism. To be rich is glorious". Poverty is not capitalism, or Christianity, or Catholicity either. Since 1978, China's reform has lifted 500 million people out of extreme poverty. In the U.S. the people below poverty lines have increased. In August 2012, The Atlantic had an article "Reform Is Not Enough: The Federal Government Needs a Complete Makeover" (Howard, 2012). Deng said, "Reform is China's second revolution." The U.S. needs a second revolution to reform or complete makeovers to overhaul its federal, state, and local government systems.

In 1980, China setup four Special economic zones with no custom duties, income taxes for years or very low taxes to lure foreign direct investments, technologies, and companies from overseas. The first four special economic zones were Shenzhen, Zhuhai and Shantou in Guangdong Province and Xiamen in Fujian Province. Shenzhen is most well known one.

In 1979, Shenzhen consisted of mostly fishing and farming villages with a population of 300,000 located near Hong Kong. Shenzhen GDP per capita was under $100 per year at that time. Thirty-four years later, Shenzhen is one of the largest cities in China with a population of over 12 million, annual $200 billion

GDP. Its GDP per capita has increased to $20,000 per year. Shenzhen is one of the major manufacturing centers in China (Shenzhen, 2013). Shenzhen created millions of jobs in Shenzhen and other places in China. That is just the effect of one city. Overall China's GDP growth from Shenzhen and other special economic zones are contributing factors for the manufacturing jobs losses in the United States and other Western countries. Today, Shenzhen and other Chinese cities are competing for USA's white-collar office, technology, legal, and medical jobs. Special Economic Zones originally started in the Western countries. Why the U.S. and other developed countries cannot try reforms and experiment ideas and polices in special zones? Governments can provide free land leasing for 50 years, and infrastructures such as highways, hospitals, and schools on federal lands for information technology companies and biotechnology companies. The Governors Island near Wall Street can be one. But larger areas would be preferred, maybe large islands, or in California.

In November 2013, entrepreneur named Balaji Srinivasan took the stage to lay out a case for Silicon Valley's independence. His idea seemed a more expansive version of Google Chief Executive Larry Page's call for setting aside "a piece of the world" to try out controversial new technologies, and investor Peter Thiel's "Seastead" movement, which aims to launch tech-utopian island nations (Manjoo, 2013).

The US Congressional Research Service published a report, "China's Economic Rise: History, Trends, Challenges, and Implications for the United States" on September 7, 2013. Prior to the initiation of economic reforms and trade liberalization 34 years ago, China maintained policies that kept the economy very poor, stagnant, centrally controlled, vastly inefficient, and relatively isolated from the global economy. Since opening up to foreign trade and investment and implementing free market reforms in 1979, China has been among the world's fastest-growing economies, with real annual gross domestic product (GDP) growth averaging nearly 10% through 2012. In recent years, China has emerged as a major global economic and trade power. It is currently the world's second-largest economy, largest merchandise exporter, second-largest merchandise importer, second-largest destination of foreign direct investment (FDI), largest manufacturer, and largest holder of foreign exchange reserves" (Morrison, 2013).

China's GDP has grown from $260 billion in 1979 to $8.2 trillion in 2012 (Morrison, 2013). China greatly improved the living standards of millions of Chinese. Because China's economy has been export driven since 1979, the gains of jobs and GDP often result in job losses and slowing or decreasing of GDPs in developed countries. As China exports more and more products and services to the West, the developed countries gave China more and more paper IOU debts because of the trade deficits. The debts stockpile higher as foreign reserves for China, currently over $3 trillion (Foreign exchange reserves of the People's Republic of China, 2013). Because of the declining of real manufacturing activities and jobs, U.S. and other western countries' financial institution moved into financial engineering, such as subprime mortgages. With increase money supplies by quantitative easing around the world, more and more money poured into mutual funds, private equities, and hedge funds. These funds moved money around the globe to chase paper profits for themselves and their clients. Sometimes, these massive speculative activities created financial bubbles, such as the 1997 Asian currency crisis, 2001 dot.com bubble, and lately 2008 financial crisis. Each time, the bets get large, the crisis gets more severe. The 2008 financial crisis caused many corporate collapse of export driven companies in coastal provinces in China. The crisis forced China try to transit its economy from export driven to internal consumer driven economy and to move up the manufacturing chain.

Manufacturers are important sectors for a healthy and strong economy even in a knowledge economy. Manufacturers offer and increase the need for services. An economy depends mainly on its service sectors is not sustainable or a healthy one. U.S. consumers have benefited from the export of cheap products from China and other countries over the years. Some sectors are somewhat immune from foreign exporters, such as housings, medical cares, hospital services, public schools, and higher educations. In the U.S., medicine related jobs, such as surgeons, anesthesiologist, and dentists, are the majority of the top 20 highest ones.

China has been a large construction site all over the country. China will be building a city bigger than Philadelphia each year for the next twenty years. There are more than 400 cities in China. More than one hundred of them have more than a million people. In twenty years, that number could double to 800 cities (Canton, 2006). The recent proposed new huge city Bohai Economic Rim will have a population of 260 million, which center on Beijing and Tianjin with high speed rail links (Chang, 2013). I often go back to China because my mother, my sister and relatives still live in China. When I go back to China, I usually visited my old friends in Kunming. Usually in a few years, these friends would get new or upgraded apartments. Although my apartment in New York City is usually more expensive than theirs in term of dollars, my place is not necessary bigger or newer than theirs. For a fraction of my home price, their places are bigger, newer, higher and with all new furniture and appliances. Their incomes usually lower than my income after converting to US dollars. They do own new cars, usually Japanese autos manufactured in China, and the same home appliances, but sometimes different brands. Because my higher price home, I got a larger mortgage loan, a much higher monthly mortgage payment for a smaller and older apartment. The electricity and water, gas prices are lower, and even lower common charge and they don't pay property taxes.

Another big expense category in the U.S. is in health care related expenses. For people with insurances, they usually don't see the actual hospitals' or doctors' invoices. They just pay the co-payments, sometimes after reaching the deductibles. In 2010, the aggregate cost for hospital stays was $375.9 billion; the average cost per stay was $9,700 (Pfuntner, Wier, Lauren, & Steiner, 2013)
.

Unless new technologies or low price products disrupt current existing companies, consumers will continue to receive products or services at much higher prices. There are lower manufactured products from China, lower priced call centers in India. The Internet and cellular phones basically wipe out the huge profits and high prices of long distance call and international calls used to be monopolized by a few companies. Word Processor ended typewriter manufactures.

Ample media reported on the U.S. government shutdown in October 2013, the debt ceiling debates, and the Obamacare. The U.S. political system, and debt crisis has reached a critical point. As Mayo Clinic' CEO John H. Noseworthy stated that Obamacare lacks key cost control (Belvedere, 2013). At current rate of spending with the entitlements such as Medicare, Medicaid, and social security, and if the national debts as percent of GDP continues to grow, the U.S. government will not able to serve its debts and may lead to default. The two-party one-person-per-vote system has created more harm for the federal, state, and local governments. Politicians are forced to become short-term focus on the current election and the next re-election. You don't have to be an able leader with track records. What is more important is packaging in a polished way and advertising. To win vote, the politician must give away more. To beat the opponents, you promise more to give away more. It is like free for all buffets. Thus America became a more welfare state, and cannot get out of this deep hole.

Philip K. Howard published an article on The Atlantic on August 3, 2102: "Reform Is Not Enough: The Federal Government Needs a Complete Makeover" (Howard, 2012). I believe that the America will be at a better place to merge the Democratic Party with the Republic Party into one political party – a Democratic Republic Party, or calling it Pro-Knowledge Party (Koenig, 2013). The world is shifting from an industrial economy towards a knowledge economy. After merging the Democrats and the Republicans, the party should make a crime for anyone who tries to break the one-party system for the national interest. Ron

Fournier published an article on the National Journal on January 14, 2013 "Talkin' about Revolution: 6 Reasons Why the Two-Party System May Become Obsolete - No Labels is a symptom of public's hunger for change, if not the final solution". Congress has formed a "Problem Solvers' Group" committee including 12 Republicans and 13 Democrats to look into the No Labels agenda (Fournier, 2013).

The U.S.A. founding fathers did not want the American to be a two-party political system (The Founding Fathers Tried to Warn Us About the Threat From a Two-Pary System, 2011). Alexander Hamilton and James Madison respectively warned the dangers of domestic political factions. George Washington was not a member of any political party. Fearing conflict and inefficiency, he hoped that political parties would not be formed. Nevertheless, the American two-party system emerged from Washington's advisors, including Hamilton and Madison.

The Economist published an article "Go East, young bureaucrat - Emerging Asia can teach the West a lot about government" on March 17th, 2011. This article suggested the Western countries to learn from the Singapore economic and government model. Singapore is a small Southeast Asian city-country founded in 1963 by Cambridge educated lawyer Lee Kuan Yew. Singapore has a population of 5 million without any natural resources. Its GDP per capita has grown from $400 in 1963 to $50,000 in 2012, a higher GDP per capita than the U.S.A (IMF Report for Selected Countries and Subjects, 2013). Singapore's average annual GDP growth rate had been about 8% from 1965 to 2006 (Siddiqui, 2010). Lee's People's Action Party (PAP) has controlled its parliament since its independence. Because PAP knows that they will win every election, so the party can take long view and be patient. As Prime Minister Lee Kuan Yew said "Our strength is that we are able to think strategically and look ahead," and "If the government changed every five years it would be harder" (Go East, young bureaucrat - Emerging Asia can teach the West a lot about government, 2011). "I ignore polling as a method of government. I think that shows a certain weakness of mind – on inability to chart a course whatever way the wind blows, whichever way the media encourage the people to go, you follow. If you can't force or are unwilling to force your people to follow you, with or without threats, you are not a leader."

Prime Minister Lee Kuan Yew has been advisor for every Chinese leader since his meeting with Deng Xiaoping in November 1978. Many heads of states consulted with him on Asian affairs. Here are appraises for Prime Minister Lee Kuan Yew from US presidents: "The fact that a leader of Lee's breath of vision was not able to act on a broad stage represents an incalculable losses to the world" - Richard Nixon. Lee "is one of the legendary figures of Asia in the 20th and 21th centuries. He is somebody who helped to trigger the Asian economic miracle" - Barack Obama. "Lee's life of public service is both unique and remarkable…His work as Prime Minister and now as Minister Mentor has helped literally millions of people in Singapore and all across Southeast Asia to live better, more prosperous lives. I hope the leaders of ASEAN (the Association of Southeast Asian Nations) will continue to build upon Mr. Lee Kuan Yew's outstanding legacy… I thank you (the U.S. – ASEAN Business Council) for honoring a man I admire so very much" - Bill Clinton. "In my long life in public service, I have encountered many bright, able people. None is more impressive than Lee Kuan Yew" (Endorsement of Lee's lifelong challenge: Singapore's Bilingual Journey, 2011) - George H. W. Bush.

Singapore has outstanding civil services. Singapore's government follows an elitist model, paying top government officials $2 million or more a year (Why Singapore Has the Cleanest Government Money Can Buy, 2012). Mr. Lee treats the government as Singapore, Inc., the largest enterprise in the country. Systems are setup to spot talents earlier, lure them with scholarships, and keeping invest in them. In justifying million-dollar pay hike for Singapore ministers, Mr. Lee said, "You know the cure for all this talk is really a good dose of incompetent government. You get that alternative and you'll never put Singapore together again: Humpty Dumpty cannot be put together again…my asset values will disappear, my apartments will be worth a fraction of what they were, my ministers' jobs will in peril, their security will be at risk and their women will become maids in other people's countries, foreign workers. I cannot have that". "I started off believing all men were equal. I now know that's the most unlikely thing ever to have been, because millions of years have passed over evolution, people have scattered across the face of this earth, been isolated from each other, developed independently, had different intermixtures between races, people, climates, soils… I didn't start off that knowledge. But by observation, reading, watching, arguing, asking, and bullying my way to the top, that's the conclusion I've come to."

What caused the failures for the Communes in China and entitlements in the United States and the many western countries was because people lost their motivations to work hard. China's reform and openness under Deng stimulated people's motivation to work hard for themselves. For most people, working and serve others, or higher goals to serve the human races under communism doctrine without proper reward systems, just do not work. A good working system needs to unlock the human potentials to increase productivity and to innovate. Money become the best method to reward people to work extra hard, to put extra hours, and to go the extra miles. As Lee Kuan Yew says, it is better for a country to give the money to the people for their housing, health care, education. It is difficult for know how much each thing cost, such as the cost of each medical procedure in health care. Government should create an environment that jobs are plentiful. People should put a portion of their hard earned money away for future expenditures to buy homes, medical expense, and education with contribution from the employers and the government.

Individual personal responsibility and individual family responsibility should be the core of any successful societies, capitalism or socialism.

Moving away from individual responsibility, persons, companies, and countries will stop growing. Examples are China's

Great Leap Forward, US' social security and Medicare woes, and Eurozone crisis. Positive examples are China's openness and reform, and Singapore's CPF (Central Provident Fund). Individual responsibilities will keep cost down and profit high. Individual, companies and countries will prosper. Governments should reallocate wealth to provide good infrastructures, education system, safe and good investment environments and affordable health care. Government should provide supports to people who have no means to take care themselves, but the number should be small.

"You're talking about Rwanda or Bangladesh, or Cambodia, or the Philippines. They've got democracy, according to Freedom House. But have you got a civilized life to lead? People want economic development first and foremost. The leaders may talk something else. You take a poll of any people. What is it they want? The right to write an editorial, as you like? They want homes, medicine, jobs, and schools." – Lee Kuan Yew

Chapter 12 Jobs: China, Inc. and U.S.A., Inc.

"Hence the saying: If you know the enemy and know yourself, you need not fear the result of a hundred battles. If you know yourself but not the enemy, for every victory gained you will also suffer a defeat. If you know neither the enemy nor yourself, you will suffer a defeat in every battle." The Art of War by Sun Tzu

"When you're Singapore's leader and your existence depends on performance – extraordinary performance, better than your competitors – when that performance disappears because the system on which it's been based becomes eroded, then you've lost everything…I try to tell the younger generation that and they say the old man is playing the same record, we've heard it all before. I happen to know how we got here and I know how we can unscramble it." – On one freak election result running Singapore, Lee Kuan Yew

The federal government is the largest enterprise of the U.S.A., with annual expenditure of $3.8 trillion, over 2.8 million civilian employees and 1.6 million military personnel in 2011. About half of the revenues of most hospitals, clinics, and physicians come from the government's Medicare and Medicaid programs. Public primary and secondary education system and colleges receive their funding from state, local, and federal governments.

Total 2013 Spending by Function

Function	
Total spending	$6.5 trillion
Pensions	$1.2 trillion
Health Care	$1.3 trillion
Education	$1.0 trillion
Defense	$0.8 trillion
Welfare	$0.5 trillion

State & Local 2014 Spending by Function

Function	
Total spending	$3.3 trillion
Pensions	$0.2 trillion
Health Care	$0.7 trillion
Education	$0.9 trillion
Welfare	$0.3 trillion
Protection	$0.2 trillion
Transport	$0.3 trillion

Source: from www.usgovernmentspending.com

Note 1: Federal spending after 2012 is budgeted. Note 2: State spending after 2011 and local spending after 2011 are "guesstimated" by projecting the latest change in reported spending forward to future years

The above data are about government jobs. How about private jobs? The U.S. federal government usually leaves the private industries alone. But in this age of global competition, is this put the U.S. businesses and U.S. in disadvantages? The answer is definitely yes.

In 2011, 35% of all China's business activity and 43 percent of all company profits come from state owned enterprises (SOEs), in which the Chinese government owns a majority interest (Government-owned corporation, 2013).

The State-owned Assets Supervision and Administration Commission (SASAC) is the government body responsible for managing 117 large SOEs (List of State-owned enterprises in China, 2013). This list does not include provincial, city, and local government owned enterprises.

1. China National Nuclear Corporation
2. China Nuclear Engineering Group Corporation
3. China Aerospace Science and Technology Corporation
4. China Aerospace Science and Industry Corporation

5. Aviation Industry Corporation of China
6. China State Shipbuilding Corporation
7. China Shipbuilding Industry Corporation
8. China North Industries Group Corporation
9. China South Industries Group Corporation
10. China Electronics Technology Group Corporation
11. China National Petroleum Corporation
12. China Petrochemical Corporation (Sinopec Group)
13. China National Offshore Oil Corporation
14. State Grid Corporation of China
15. China Southern Power Grid Company
16. China Huaneng Group
17. China Datang Corporation
18. China Huadian Corporation
19. China Guodian Corporation
20. China Power Investment Corporation
21. China Three Gorges Corporation
22. Shenhua Group Corporation Limited
23. China Telecommunications Corporation
24. China Unicom
25. China Mobile Communications Corporation
26. China Electronics Corporation
27. China FAW Group Corporation
28. Dongfeng Motor Corporation
29. China First Heavy Industries
30. China National Erzhong Group Co.
31. Harbin Electric Corporation

32. Dongfang Electric Corporation
33. Anshan Iron and Steel Group Corporation
34. Baosteel Group Corporation
35. Wuhan Iron and Steel (Group) Corporation
36. Aluminum Corporation of China
37. China Ocean Shipping (Group) Company
38. China Shipping (Group) Company
39. China National Aviation Holding Company
40. China Eastern Air Holding Company
41. China Southern Air Holding Company
42. Sinochem Group
43. COFCO Limited
44. China Minmetals Corporation
45. China General Technology (Group) Holding, Limited
46. China State Construction Engineering Corporation
47. China Grain Reserves Corporation
48. State Development & Investment Corp.
49. China Merchants Group
50. China Resources
51. China National Travel Service (HK) Group Corporation [China Travel Service (Holdings) Hong Kong Limited]
52. State Nuclear Power Technology Corporation Ltd
53. Commercial Aircraft Corporation of China, Ltd
54. China Energy Conservation and Environmental Protection Group

55. China International Engineering Consulting Corporation
56. China Huafu Trade & Development Group Corp
57. China Chengtong Holdings Group Ltd
58. China National Coal Group Corp
59. China Coal Technology & Engineering Group Corp
60. China National Machinery Industry Corporation
61. China Academy of Machinery Science & Technology
62. Sinosteel Corporation
63. China Metallurgical Group Corporation
64. China Iron & Steel Research Institute Group
65. China National Chemical Corporation
66. China National Chemical Engineering Group Corporation
67. Sinolight Corporation
68. China National Arts & Crafts (Group) Corporation
69. China National Salt Industry Corporation
70. Huacheng Investment & Management Co., Ltd
71. China Hengtian Group Co., Ltd
72. China National Materials Group Corporation Ltd
73. China National Building Materials Group Corporation
74. China Nonferrous Metal Mining (Group) Co., Ltd
75. General Research Institute for Nonferrous Metals
76. Beijing General Research Institute of Mining & Metallurgy
77. China International Intellectech Corporation

78. China Academy of Building Research
79. China North Locomotive and Rolling Stock Industry (Group) Corporation
80. China South Locomotive & Rolling Stock Corporation Limited
81. China Railway Signal & Communication Corporation
82. China Railway Group Limited
83. China Railway Construction Corporation Limited
84. China Communications Construction Company Limited
85. Potevio Company Limited
86. China Academy of Telecommunication and Technology
87. China National Agricultural Development Group Co., Ltd
88. Chinatex Corporation
89. Sinotrans & CSC Holdings Co., Ltd
90. China National Silk Import & Export Corporation
91. China Forestry Group Corporation
92. China National Pharmaceutical Group Corporation
93. CITS Group Corporation
94. China Poly Group Corporation
95. Zhuhai ZhenRong Company
96. China Architecture Design & Research Group
97. China Metallurgical Geology Bureau
98. China National Administration of Coal Geology
99. Xinxing Cathay International Group Co., Ltd

100. China Travelsky Holding Company
101. China National Aviation Fuel Group Corporation
102. China Aviation Supplies Holding Company
103. Power Construction Corporation of China
104. China Energy Engineering Group Co., Ltd
105. China National Gold Group Corporation
106. China National Cotton Reserves Corporation
107. China Printing (Group) Corporation
108. China Guangdong Nuclear Power Holding Corporation Ltd
109. China Hualu Group Co., Ltd
110. Alcatel-Lucent Shanghai Bell Co., Ltd
111. IRICO Group Corporation
112. Wuhan Research Institute of Post and Telecommunications
113. OCT Group
114. Nam Kwong (Group) Company Limited
115. China XD Group
116. China Railway Materials Commercial Corp
117. China Reform Holdings Corporation Ltd

The United States-China Economic and Security Review Commission also includes large State-owned banks and insurance companies not managed by the State-owned Assets Supervision and Administration Commission (SASAC) as part of its list of large central SOE in its 2012 annual report to Congress:

- Industrial & Commercial Bank of China ICBC
- China Life Insurance Group China Life
- China Construction Bank CCD
- Bank of China BOC

- Agriculture Bank of China
- China Taiping Insurance Group Company China Taiping
- Bank of Communications BOCOM
- China Development Bank CDB
- People's Insurance Company of China PICC

Many large SOEs are non-public listed companies, so their financial information is not disclosed. Some SOEs only have subsidiaries listed on stock exchanges. In 1996, only two Chinese companies were on the Fortune Global 500 list with combined revenues of $31.6 billion (Fortune Global 500, 1996). 17 years later, in 2013, 89 Chinese companies on Fortune Global 500 list with combined revenues of $5.0 trillion (Fortune Global 500, 2013):

1996

Fortune 500 List Rank	Company Name	Revenues ($ billion)	Profits ($ billion)
167	Bank of China	19.3	0.9
338	COFCO	12.3	0.1
	Total	31.6	1.0

2013

Fortune 500 List Rank	Company Name	Revenues ($ billion)	Profits ($b.)
4	Sinopec Group	428.2	8.2
5	China National Petroleum	408.6	18.2
7	State Grid	298.4	12.3
29	Industrial Bank of China	133.6	37.8
50	China Construction Bank	113.4	30.6
64	Agricultural Bank of China	103.5	23.0
70	Bank of China	98.4	22.1
71	China Mobile	96.9	11.9
76	Noble Group	94.0	0.5
80	China State Construction	90.6	1.3
93	China National Offshore Oil	83.5	7.7
100	China Railway Construction	77.2	0.8
102	China Railway Group	76.7	1.2
103	SAIC Motor7	6.2	3.3

111	China Life Insurance	73.7	-1.7
119	Sinochem Group	71.8	0.8
134	China Southern Power Grid	66.7	1.0
141	China FAW Group	64.9	2.6
146	Dongfeng Motor Group	61.7	1.3
161	China North Industries	58.0	0.7
172	CITIC Group	55.4	4.8
178	Shenhua Group	54.5	6.2
181	Ping An Insurance	53.8	3.2
182	China Telecommunications	53.4	1.1
187	China Resources National	52.4	1.9
192	China Minmetals	51.8	0.7
196	China Post Group	50.9	4.1
209	China South Industries	48.0	0.2
212	Aviation Industry Corp.	47.4	1.0
213	China Communications	47.3	1.2
222	Baosteel Group	45.7	0.9
231	China Huaneng Group	44.3	0.1
243	Bank of Communications	43.1	9.3
256	People's Insurance Co.	40.8	1.1
258	China United Network	40.6	0.4
266	Jardine Matheson	39.6	1.7
269	HeBei Iron & Steel Group	39.3	-0.2
273	Aluminum Corp. of China	38.8	-0.8
277	China National Aviation Fuel	38.4	0.1
292	China Railway Materials	37.2	0.1
299	China Guodian	36.8	0.2
302	China Metallurgical Group	36.8	-0.8
311	Jizhong Energy Group	35.3	0.1
315	Huawei Investment	34.9	2.4
318	Jiangsu Shagang Group	34.6	0.1
319	China National Building	34.5	0.5
322	Shougang Group	34.3	0.1
326	Sinomach	34.0	0.7
328	Wuhan Iron & Steel	33.9	0.0
329	Lenovo Group	33.9	0.6
336	Beijing Automotive Group	33.4	1.1
343	Tewoo Group	32.9	0.1

354	Power China	32.0	0.7
355	ChemChina	32.0	-0.2
357	COFCO	31.8	0.6
359	Greenland Holding Group	31.7	1.2
363	Hutchison Whampoa	31.3	3.4
364	Zhejiang Materials Industry	31.2	0.0
373	Shandong Energy Group	30.7	0.9
376	China Datang	30.4	-0.1
387	Amer International Group	29.6	0.6
388	Shandong Weiqiao	29.6	1.1
389	China Huadian	29.3	0.5
390	Shanxi Coal Transportation	29.3	0.0
395	China Electronics	29.0	0.2
401	China Ocean Shipping	28.7	-0.4
403	Shanxi Coking Coal Group	28.6	0.0
404	Henan Coal & Chemical	28.6	-0.4
406	Xinxing Cathay International	28.6	0.3
407	Yangquan Coal Industry	28.6	0.0
408	China Power Investment	28.6	0.2
411	China Minsheng Banking	28.4	6.0
412	China Merchants Bank	28.0	7.2
414	Jiangxi Copper	27.9	0.3
415	Kailuan Group	27.8	0.1
417	China Shipbuilding Industry	27.8	1.0
428	Industrial Bank	27.2	5.5
429	China Pacific Insurance	27.2	0.8
430	Shanxi LuAn Mining Group	27.1	0.0
432	Datong Coal Mine Group	27.0	-0.1
435	Shanxi Jincheng Anthracite	26.8	0.3
446	Sinopharm	26.2	0.3
460	Shanghai Pudong Develop	25.4	5.4
464	Shaanxi Yanchang Petroleum	25.3	2.4
466	Bailian Group	25.2	0.1
477	Zhejiang Geely Holding	24.6	0.1
482	China Nonferrous Metal	24.1	0.1
483	Guangzhou Automobile	24.1	0.1
493	Ansteel Group	<u>23.6</u>	<u>-1.6</u>
	Total	4,957.30	262.4

Source: Fortune 2013 Global 500 List.

Usually employee salary expenses are about 33 percent of company's revenues for non-service companies and 50 percent of company's revenue for a service company (Wayne, 2013). Let us assuming that companies use 40 percent revenues to cover employee salaries. For the 89 Chinese companies on the 2013 Fortune Global 500 listed above, $1.9 trillion can be used for employees' payroll. According to World Bank, China's gross national income per capita of $6,091 ranked 90th in the world in 2012. Let assume that the average paycheck per year is $6,091 per employee, thus $1.9 trillion translates to 312 million jobs every year. US Bureau of Labor Statistics reported that the US labor force is 155 million with 144 million people employed, a 7.3 percent unemployment rate as of August 2013. So the 89 Chinese SOEs probably employ about twice the people of the entire US labor force.

The Sovereign Wealth Fund Institute indicates that China Investment Corporation, SAFE Investment Company, and National Social Security Fund China are three of the largest Sovereign Funds in the world. In 2013, China Investment Corporation has $575.2 billion assets under management, and SAFE Investment Company has $567.9 billion, and National Social Security Fund has $160.6 billion (Sovereign Wealth Fund Rankings, 2013). These three funds with over $1.3 trillion in assets invest in key technology industries and foster growth of invested companies. Back in 1980, China's GDP was $202 billion according to World Bank data.

A government's most important functions should be creating jobs, providing decent housing, good health care, and good education to its citizens. For a decade or two, the US government has been stimulating economy using lowering interest rate or printing money. But the Fed interest rate is close to zero, and has no room for future decreasing. Printing more money will cause inflation. Without creating real jobs, governmental financial engineering only decreasing people's real living standards. A government's jobs should not be just collecting taxes from people who work and redistributing the money to create welfares to people who do not work. The wonderful monetary reward system is a double edged sword. The monetary reward system can defeat the communism, but the same reward system can also drown the capitalism if a country moves towards a welfare state.

South Korea is one of the four Asian Tiger countries. Top ten chaebol in Korea now almost accounts 80 percent of Korean economy (Top ten chaebol now almost 80% of Korean economy, 2012). Chaebols are family controlled conglomerates with tight governmental supports and favors.

Here are Korea's Corporate Heavyweights (Yoon, 2012):
(1) Samsung Group
Total Sales in 2012: $245.7 billion
Samsung Electronics, Samsung Heavy Industries, Samsung Engineering, Samsung SDI and Samsung Display
(2) Hyundai Kia Automotive Group
Total Sales in 2012: $140.7 billion
Hyundai Motor, Kia Motors, Hyundai Steel, Hyundai Hysco, Hyundai Mobis
(3) SK Group
Total Sales in 2012: $139.8 billion
SK Hynix, SK Innovation, SK Telecom, SK Engineering & Construction
(4) LG Group
Total Sales in 2012: $100.6 billion
LG Electronics, LG Display, LG Telecom, LG Chem
(5) Lotte Group
Total Sales in 2012: $49.7 billion
Lotte Confectionery, Lotte Shopping, Honam Petrochemical

Samsung Electronics mobile unit's annual profit alone is more than the total profit of Google Company's annual profit based on Samsung Electronics 2012 Annual Report and Yahoo! Finance data. Samsung Group's Samsung Electronics is world's largest information technology company measured by 2012 revenues, and 4th in market value. Samsung Heavy Industries is the world's 2nd-largest shipbuilder measured by 2010 revenues (Samsung, 2013). China sends envoys to study what makes the Samsung trick in the same way that it sends its bureaucrats to learn efficient government from Singapore (Samsung and its attractions Asia's new model company, 2011). China has the all powerful National Development and Reform Commission. The U.S. government should establish an Office and allocate a power and budget to study the companies top companies like Samsung and governments like Singapore around the globe.

Government-linked corporations dominate Singapore's economy, producing as much as 60 percent of the country's GDP. These corporations include Temasek Holdings, Government of Singapore Investment Corporation, Singapore Airlines, CapitaLand, MediaCorp, Neptune Orient Lines, PSA International, Singapore Pools, Singapore Post, Singapore Power, SingTel, SMRT Corporation, and ST Engineering. According to the Sovereign Wealth Fund Institute, Government of Singapore Investment Corporation and Temasek Holdings are two of the largest ten Sovereign Funds in the world, with $248 billion and $157 billion under management in 2012 (Sovereign Wealth Fund Rankings, 2013). It is an amazing achievement for a city nation of 5 million people and with no natural resources of its own. These two funds strategically invest and forester key technology industry and companies around the world.

Singapore's government provides a good model, and China has been more or less following Singapore's model. The most important aspects of Singapore Model are the Central Provident Fund (CPF) and state owned enterprises. In Singapore, the Central Provident Fund is mandatory defined contribution comprehensive savings accounts for working citizens and permanent residents to accumulate funds primarily for their housing, health care, and family education needs. According the Central Provident Fund Board, as of June 2013, CPF has 3.5 million members with a positive balance of S$243 billion. The CPF was started in July 1955 when the British controlled the colony. The employee contributes 20 percent of his monthly gross salary while employer contributes 16% of his salary (Central Provident Fund - Ministry of Manpower, 2013).

In the U.S., you are probably familiar with the defined contribution pension plans, such as Traditional or Roth Individual Retirement Account (IRA) and 401(k). Both the employee and the employer contribute to these kinds of pension plans. The employer only guarantees the contribution to the accounts, but do not guarantee the future benefits or future values. Future values are based on contribution and investment performances. Some profitable and rich companies may still have defined benefits pension plans, or get stuck with defined benefits plans with earlier employees involuntarily. That is one reason that the US auto industries, many companies, and some county governments filed bankruptcy.

The Medicare and social security are defined benefit programs. The federal government guarantees the workers for these entitlements no matter what the fiscal condition of the government. But with the coming baby boomers' record retirements, the federal government will face tough times in the future. According to Social Security Administration, the Social Security Fund will run out of money in 2033. Medicare's trust fund will be depleted in 2024 (SSA, 2013). The social security and Medicare funds are counting on the current workers to pay for the retirement and health care expenses of old individuals. However, when social security was established the life expectance was 65, so the government did not expect most people to collect any retirement money. As the life expectancy increase, the retirement system barely changed.

The social security and Medicare funds only work if the working population will be stable or continuously increase and life expectance do not increase. Such a system is not going to work under current conditions. Somehow the social security and Medicare run like Ponzi schemes using new comers' money to pay members who were in earlier (Salsman, 2011; Conover, 2011).

But if you live long than 2024 or 2033, it likely that you won't see a penny for Medicare or social security based on current depletion rate. After the financial crisis in 2008, many corporations and organizations in the U.S. have switched from defined benefit retirement plans to defined contribution plans such as 401(k), particularly for new employees. As the largest enterprise in the U.S., it is time for the federal government to take the hard medicine and take a careful look at how to reform the social security pooled insurance fund and pooled Medicare insurance fund, and transition to individually responsible long-long assets savings contribution retirement accounts and full medical savings accounts.

The federal government can get money through two ways. One way is collecting taxes from individuals and companies. Another way is borrowing from the public and other countries by issuing U.S. treasuries bills, notes, and bonds. Currently, the federal government has debts of over $16 trillion, which is more the U.S.'s GDP. Although U.S. can keep selling treasury notes and bonds, at certain points the demands will decrease. The interest rates will increase if the total national debts go much higher against GDP. Rating agencies around the world will downgrade U.S.'s national credit ratings. This happened to Greece, Spain, Iceland, and Portugal during Eurozone debt crisis.

When Singapore became independent in 1965, there was very little money in the Central Provident Fund (CPF). Half of the people had no homes lived in refugee conditions, and the country had a high unemployment rate. The CPF accounts are lifelong assets accounts. Money in the CPF accounts come from Singaporeans' salaries and contribution from employers. Money is under individual control. The CPF will be used for their retirement, health care, and children education expenses. The government will not mail each one a social security check, although individuals are encouraged to purchase annuities. Medical expenses will also come from your CPF accounts, although Singapore government recommends people to purchase additional catastrophic medical insurances. People can buy government public housings using the CPF as down payments. Although the prices of public housings are 50 percent to 70 percent below market prices, the high-rise public housings are in great quality. 85 percent of Singaporeans live in these purchased public housings (Yuen, 2007). Singaporeans have the 4th highest life expectance in the world, and are living considerable healthy lives (CIA The World Factbook, 2013).

The CPF accounts create flows of cash for the government, just like insurance companies. The money in CPF accounts belongs to individuals, but they probably won't use the money for retirement or major medical expenses for next 30 years. Majority of people's medical expenses usually occur during the last few years of their life. The Singapore government has been using the cheap money from CPF accounts to develop infrastructures and housing.

Unions

"The secret to success is to do the common things uncommonly well." -- John D. Rockefeller

Immediately after independence, Singapore nationalized all labor unions by requiring all unions to register with National Trade Union Congress. The dominant People's Action Party normally appoints the General Secretary of the Union Congress. If workers go on strikes, the workers would lose their jobs. The government stresses that with no natural resources of its own, lack of cooperation from workers means withdrawal of foreign direct investment and developments. By nationalizing the unions, Singapore can keep the labor wages low and competitive (Han, 2012). China allows limited union activities.

Many believed that unions bankrupted the U.S. auto industry. The Heritage Foundation published an article: "UAW Workers Actually Cost the Big Three Automakers $70 an Hour" (Sherk, 2008). The big three automakers cannot fire union workers, and have to pay a non-working union workers over

$100,000 a year in pay and benefits. First, the quality of the cars can be in question because less motivated and less productive workers. Second, how can American cars compete in prices with foreign cars with the drags of big union pensions? The woes of the big three auto makers subsequently led to the bankruptcy of the City of Detroit. Normally the wages and salaries are 30 to 50 percent of a company's revenues. With extra costs of benefits, labor expense is a big portion of a company's operation cost. With USA labor costs ranked near the top of the world, any more increases of pays will deter foreign investments, and push companies go overseas. The unions and employees need to understand that in this knowledge / innovation economy, owners and employers have much less control over the markets. In a natural resources or industrial dominated economy, it was easier to monopolize an industry. Customers pay the employees' salaries, not the bosses. The customers can always buy from other companies for products and services. With increasing globalization, customers can buy products and services from other countries. If you research troubled companies, you will find labor problems often trigger and speeded up the downfalls of companies and organization. With my suggested merge of the Demarcates and the Republics, the one party can curtail the labor costs to make US companies more competitive. Workers and corporations will both win as a result.

"I believe in the dignity of labor, whether with head or hand; that the world owes no man a living but that it owes every man an opportunity to make a living." -- John D. Rockefeller

Chapter 13 Home Ownerships and Health Care

"I am often accused of interfering in the private lives of citizens. Yes, I did not, had I not done that, we wouldn't be here today. And I say without the slightest remorse, that we wouldn't be here, we would not have made economic progress, if we had not intervened on very personal matters – who your neighbor is, how you live, the noise you make, how you spit, or what language you use. We decide what is right, never mind what the people think." – Lee Kuan Yew, Prime Minister of Singapore

90% of Singaporeans own a home, whereas 65% of Americans own a home (Callis & Kresin, 2013). According to Singapore's Housing and Development Board, 85 percent of the Singaporeans, or 8 in 10 residence population live in public housings. When Singapore became independent, the home ownership percentage was low, with many people lived in slums and squatters. Living in a public housing in Singapore is generally not considered a sign of poverty or lower standard of living, as compared to public housings in other countries.

Public housings in Singapore are built with a variety of quality and styles to cater the middle and upper income groups. Singapore's public housings are usually apartment buildings, and high rises especially the newer ones, located in housing estates. Each housing estate is a self-contained satellite town with schools, supermarkets, clinics, restaurant centers, and sports and recreation facilities (Public housing in Singapore, 2013).

Singapore's public housing apartment prices are 50 percent to 70 percent cheaper than comparable privately developed apartments. How does Singapore build such housings without create large burdens to the government finance? Three factors are important contributing factors: land prices, cheap funds from Central Provident Fund and subsidies from government surpluses (Yuen, 2007).

Land price is a major development cost in city-state such as Singapore or major metropolitans, such as Manhattan, Tokyo, and Hong Kong. After becoming independent, Singapore made housing ownership a duty of the government. The government believes that owning a house is a necessary item for a family, as educations, medicines, and jobs. In 1966, Singapore passed Land Acquisition Act. Under the Act, the government can compulsorily acquire any private use or commercial use land for the public interest. The government pays the owners of the land, determined by the government, and usually much lower than the market price. This approach has helped the government to lower the costs of housings. Now, 85 percent of the land is owned by the Singapore government. With a majority of the country's land, Singapore government can keep the land price relatively low. It took government decades to get here, but the long term benefits to its citizens are great.

In the U.S., the government can seize or purchase a private land based on public interest, usually for highway construction under eminent domain law (Eminent domain, 2013). Eminent domain law seldom applies to public housing constructions. Few people benefit from high land prices, except few large land and real estate owners. A University of Chicago research indicated that 18.5 Million U.S. households pay more than half their income for housing, therefore reducing money available for other necessities. Living standard decreased because you are living in much smaller apartments, old apartments because of the high home prices. People can live in larger houses in far away houses, but the daily commute can be painfully long, another living standard lowering factor. The new world trend is the increasing urbanization, which more people will live in the cities near working places, transportations, schools, doctors, and other facilities. One factor for the increasing urbanization is the rising of energy prices; another is the development of modern construction technologies for high-rise buildings.

Building constructions create jobs. Nine percent of Singapore's GDP is coming from housing construction and development (Yuen, 2007). In the U.S., the housing stocks are old. Many houses and buildings are constructed before World War II, and are still in use. Some reports claim as many as 24 new cities go up each year in China. Since 1995, China has built 129 million new urban homes (McFarlane, 2013). Building cities has created enormous construction related jobs. The whole China is like a giant construction site. Building constructions booms has been brought along the related industry developments in steel, cooper, concrete, construction materials, construction equipment, elevator, lighting, furniture, home electronics, energy, architect, etc. For example, steel and cooper brought along the mining industry, road constructions, and heavy machinery industry. Sometimes, my friends from China visited me in New York City. They were surprised to find out that the building I live in was built in the 1970s, especially an architect friend. These kinds of buildings would have been flatted for newer and high rises. The costs to rebuild are just prohibitive in the U.S.

The second measure Singapore took to lower the housing prices is utilization of Central Provident Fund. As I mentioned earlier, CPF creates cash floats similar to insurance companies. Government pays the holders of CPF about 4 percentage interests to use the cheap money to tackle infrastructure and public housings (Central Provident Fund - Ministry of Manpower, 2013). In the U.S., social security uses your social security tax to pay someone else social security checks. The social security fund will run out of money in 2033. You and I maybe not see any of our social security checks after paying the fund all of working life with government promises. This Ponzi like systems with money running out in the near future can make many people upset and angry. The Singapore's state capitalism seems more promising.

Singapore government further subsidizes its citizens through low interest mortgage loans and government grants for public housing constructions. Most newly built public housings are fully renovated. Some of the newer public housings are luxury by many standards. One new complex has eight 50 story fully renovated high rises, connected by roof top garden walk ways with full ocean and city views. Because of the government fiscal surplus and investment gains from state owned enterprises, the government can provide grants to subsidize the construction costs of public housings, further reducing the home prices. This translates to higher living standards to citizens.

Health Care

U.S. has the highest health care expenses in absolute dollars and in percentage of GDP, but not necessary better results. Here are selected countries' health care expenditure as a percentage of GDP and overall life expectancy.

Country	Health Care Expenditure of total % of GDP (2011, The World Bank)	Overall Life Expectancy (2011, World Health Organization)
United States	17.9%	79
Canada	11.2%	82
United Kingdom	9.3%	80
Japan	9.3%	83
China	5.2%	76
Singapore	4.6%	85

Note: Smoking in China is prevalent, as China is the world's largest consumer and producer of tobacco. There are estimated 350 million Chinese smokers, and China produces 42% of the world's cigarettes (Smoking in China, 2013).

According to Centers for Medicare & Medicaid Services (CMS), U.S. health care spending reached $2.7 trillion in 2011, or $8,680 per person.

Here are a National Health Expenditure 2011 Highlights from CMS:

Type or Product	Billion
Hospital Care	$850.6
Physician and Clinical Services	$541.4
Other Professional Services	$73.2
Dental Services	$108.4
Other Health, Residential, and	$133.1

Personal Care Service	
Home Health Care	$74.3
Nursing Care Facilities and Continuing Care Retirement Communities	$149.3
Prescription Drugs	$263.0
Durable Medical Equipment: Retail	$38.9
Other Non-durable Medical Products: Retail	$47.0

Health Spending by Major Funds in 2011

Funds	Billion
Medicare	$554.3
Medicaid	$407.7
Private Health Insurance	$896.3
Out-of-pocket	$307.7

Data from Centers for Medicare & Medicaid Services

In 2008, the American Magazine published an article: "The Singapore Model - The city-state of Singapore may have a fix for America's healthcare woes" (Callick, 2008). The Singaporeans are considerably healthier than the Americans, and the health care spending per person is only 20 percent of the American. In 2013, Bloomberg ranked Hong Kong and Singapore the 1st and 2nd places of the World Most Efficient Health Care. USA was ranked 46th (Bloomberg, 2013).

Singapore's health care uses Medical Savings Accounts (MSA), which is different from the MSA in the U.S. Singaporeans pay medical services from MSA. In 1984, Singapore was the first country in the world to introduce MSA to finance health care expenses. The health care system in Singapore consists of three components (the so called 3 Ms – Medisave, Medishield, and Medifund). All working families have Medisave and Medishield accounts (Schreyogg & Lim, 2004).

According to Central Intelligence Agency, Singapore's GDP per capita was US$61,400, and US' GDP per capital was US$50,700 in 2012 (CIA The World Factbook, 2013). One Singapore dollar equals 0.81 US dollar in October 2013. So at this exchange rate, Singapore's GDP per capita of US$61,400 equals to S$75,802 per year or S$6,316.8 per month using the 0.81 exchange rate. Suppose a Singapore worker makes S$4,000 a month, 16 percent of the pay, or S$640, must be paid to the Central Provident Fund. The employers must contribute 20 percent, or S$800, to the worker's CPF. In total, 36 percent of the salary will be contributed to CPF account, or S$1,440 is deposited into this worker's CPF account.

Depending on this worker's age, of the S$1,440 in CPF are divided and put into sub-accounts: between 19 – 23 percent of the 36 percent, or S$760.0 to S$920.0, goes to ordinary account for investments. Between 7 – 9 percent of the 36 percent, or S$280.0 to 360.0, goes to Medisave Account for health care expenses. Between 6 - 8 percent of the 36 percent of CPF, or S$240.0 to S$320.0, goes to Special Account for pension purpose. Governmental mandatory investment account is the largest of account of the CPF (Schreyogg & Lim, 2004). Assume this worker belongs to the 23, 7, and 6 percentage category. The yearly total contributions to the Ordinary, Medisave, and Special accounts will be S$11,040, S$3,360, and S$2,880 respectively. With the assumption of no increase in pay, no withdrawals, and without counting interest incomes, in 4 years, the total balance for the Ordinary, Medisave, and Special accounts will be S$44,160, S$13,440, and S$11,520 respectively.

If the spouse is working and making the same income, the spouse and spouse's employer must contribute the same amount if they are both in the same age group. Then in 4 years, the family's total balance for the Ordinary, Medisave, and Special accounts will be S$88,320, S$26,880, and S$23,040 respectively. If a new renovated 3-bedroom apartment in a high-rise public housing sells for S$300,000, and it requires 20 percent (S$60,000) as down payment, the couple can use S$60,000 of the S$88,320 in the CPF

Ordinary Account for the down payment. 10 percent down payment is also available. Matching twenty percent of each paycheck from the employer is mandatory investment savings, which help this family in the long run. In the US, employers must pay employees' Medicare and Social Security, but the money is deposited to the federal government not individuals' accounts and is not invested.

In the U.S. there are no forced savings. Medicare and Social Security taxes are withheld and deposited into government-pooled funds, not individual investment accounts. For employees, the Social Security tax rate is 6.2 percent on income under $113,700 through the end of 2013. Medicare tax rate is 1.45 percent of all income; for employers, the Social Security tax rate is 6.2 percent. Medicare tax rate is 1.45 percent (Social Security and Medicare tax rates; maximum taxable earnings, 2013). The combined total of 15.3 percent in the U.S. is less than the 36 percent in Singapore, but the nature of payroll taxes and Central Provident Account are different. Conservative budgeting pays.

Here are Selected Countries' Tax Rates (List of countries by tax rates, 2013)

Country /Region	Corporate tax	Individual (min)	Individual (max)	Payroll tax (usually reduces taxable income)
China	25%	5%	45%	
Hong Kong	17%	0%	15%	5% mandatory personal defined contribution pension. 40% of Hong Kong Government revenue is from indirect taxation such

				as land revenue & investment income
Japan	38%	5%	50% (40% national + 10% local)	26%
Singapore	17%-19%	4%	20%	
Switzerland	25%-13%	0%	13.2% (federal)	
United Kingdom	24%-20% (decrease to 21% in 2014), further decreased to 20% from 1 April 2015	0%	45%	25.8%-0% (National Insurance)

Singapore government also gives homebuyers subsidized mortgage loans using tax revenues. The mortgage loan interest rate was at 2.5 percent in October 2013 (Housing & Development Board, 2013). The mortgage payment will be S$1,076.68 per month, or S$12,920.16 per year, for a 25-year S$240,000 mortgage loan with a 2.5 percent rate. The monthly mortgage payment will be easy for the couple with a monthly combined income of S$8,000. They can use the money in the CPF Ordinary Account to pay for the monthly mortgage payment. The forced savings in CPF is good for families and a country's economic developments.

The money paid into CPF accounts are invested by the government. The government pays 2.5 percent interest for Ordinary Account and 4.0 percent for Medisave and Special Account as of October 2013 (Central Provident Fund - Ministry of

Manpower, 2013). As soon as the balance reaches S$30,000 in Medisave account, all future payments are automatically transferred to this individual's CPF ordinary account. Individual can leave all CPF accounts to his or her descendants. In the US, one must estimates future MSA expenses. Any unused balance will be forfeited. A new Treasury Department rule allows US$500 to be carried over to next year with many restrictions (Ebeling, 2013).

The second component of the Singapore's health care system is the Medishield, a mandatory high-risk catastrophic insurance. It is intended for expensive hospital treatments and chronic out-patient treatments. People can use Medisave account funds to purchase Medishield insurance. Private insurance companies can make profits from Singapore's health care system, but a small portion of the total health care costs. The third component of Singapore's health care system is Medifund, an endowment fund. Medifund is intended to guarantee minimum health care services for people who do not have any savings in Medisave or Medishield insurance. Certain hospital treatment and beds are subsidized by the government. For example private hospital rooms receive no subsides, while government subsidizes 80 percentage open ward beds (Schreyogg & Lim, 2004).

There have been many studies on the cause and effects of the Singapore health care costs. When the government gives individual money to buy medical services, the individual responsibility results in lowered health care costs and better health outcomes. In the U.S., the health care industry is complex and confusing. The customers (patients) usually do not pay the sellers (doctors, test services, and hospitals) directly. Customers buy or receive insurance from third parties: health-care insurance companies, Medicare, and state administrated Medicaid. Third parties review, approve, and pay the medical bills. Most customers do not know how much each visit, procedure, surgery, hospital stay costs, or care how much each costs. They just pay monthly premiums, and co-payments. Purchased services are separated from payments. Insurance companies pooled the risk in pools. This method often results in unnecessary visits and procedures.

Potential conflict of interests can exist. Doctors and hospitals are paid for treatments and procedures, not wellness of patients. Healthy and well patients sometimes mean less current and future income and business for the health care system. Physicians and hospitals sometimes have no incentives to see patients healthy and well. Even the hospitals are moving towards insurance company models, individuals are not burdened with their own health responsibilities.

The complex health care system created windfalls for certain groups. The U.S. health care expenses are $2.6 trillion a year, or 19 percentage of GDP, the highest in the world. Most of the highest paid jobs in the U.S. are for physicians, surgeons, and dentists. Senior executives are making millions a year in pharmaceutical companies, medical equipment companies, and health insurance companies. Patients, employers, and tax payers ended up footing the bills. The Medicare Fund will run out of cash in 2024. What are we going to do then? Americans are not getting healthier, or getting better medical treatments. Health care industry spent millions a year lobbying Washington, playing the two-party election politics to keep their status quo. Average American working families are working hard to make ends meals, because the higher housing costs, high health care costs are eating away the earnings.

In the long run, high health care costs cause increase in wages, and decrease workforce competitiveness, and gradually take away jobs from the U.S. workers. U.S. has lost most of its manufacturing jobs to China and other Asian countries. Now, U.S. is in danger of losing more and more white-color jobs. U.S. labor market has not fully recovered yet. People try hard, but hard to find good jobs. Even with jobs, the incomes can hardly keep up with high and increasing housing costs, health care costs and education costs. In Singapore, most people pay for their medical services out of their own savings – CPF, Medisave account, or their own bank account. Magically this system actually results in lower health care costs, better health, long life spans, and higher living standards.

Because individuals have responsibilities over the retirement savings and the medical savings accounts, Singapore's government ends up with surplus in both retirement and medical savings accounts. As a result of the surpluses, Singapore can afford to lower tax rates for both corporations and individuals. The lowered tax rates attract more and larger multinational corporations to Singapore, and create more jobs. It creates a beneficial cycle.

"Take action to fulfill your destiny, even if at first you think you suck. You just need to believe that you are Special. And in pursuing your path, you may just discover awesomeness – or attractiveness – is who you really are; and there is no charge for that!" -- Kung Fu Panda

"If you want to go fast, go alone. If you want to go far, go together" -- Richard Branson

Chapter 14 STEM Fields, High-Techs and Entrepreneurships

"Evolution moves towards greater complexity, greater elegance, greater knowledge, greater intelligence, greater beauty, greater creativity, and greater levels of subtle attributes such as love. In every monotheistic tradition God is likewise described as all of these qualities, only without limitation: infinite knowledge, infinite intelligence, infinite beauty, infinite creativity, infinite love, and so on. Of course, even the accelerating growth of evolution never achieves an infinite level, but as it explodes exponentially it certainly moves rapidly in that direction. So evolution moves inexorably towards this conception of God, although never quite reaching this ideal. We can regard, therefore, the freeing of our thinking from the severe limitations of its biological form to be an essentially spiritual undertaking." -- Ray Kurzweil

Singapore's Ministry of Trade and Industry (MTI) describes its agency: "We aim to promote sustained and inclusive economic growth, to create good quality jobs and support higher standards of living for Singaporeans. Together with our statutory boards, MTI will strive to ensure that Singapore will continue to be a city of opportunities, where people and enterprises can grow and succeed".

Ministry of Trade and Industry (MTI) promotes economic growth and create jobs, so as to achieve higher standards of living for all by: Facilitating the development of industry sectors with strong growth potential and fundamentals; Protecting Singapore's international trade interests, in particular, with a view to enhance access to global markets for our goods, services and investments; and Providing a good understanding of the current state of and outlook for the Singapore economy for policy formulation and refinement (About MTI, 2013).

Since 1978, China has also made significant investments in scientific research and technology, spending over US$100 billion on scientific research and development in 2011 alone. Science and technology are seen as vital for achieving economic and political goals, and are held as a source of national pride. Recent Chinese leaders mostly have science or technology degrees, so to a degree sometimes Chinese system is described as "techno-nationalism". Most bright college students go into science and technology fields (China, 2013).

China is rapidly developing its education system with an emphasis on science, technology, engineering, and mathematics (STEM). According to CNN, in 2009, it produced over 10,000 Ph.D. engineering graduates, and as many as 500,000 Bachelor of Science graduates, more than any other country (Colvin, 2010). China is also the world's second-largest publisher of scientific papers, producing 121,500 in 2010 alone, including 5,200 in leading international scientific journals (An, 2011). Chinese technology companies such as Huawei and Lenovo have become world leaders in telecommunications and personal computing, and Chinese supercomputers are consistently ranked among the most powerful in the world. China is furthermore the world's largest investor in renewable energy technology.

The Chinese space program is one of the world's most active, and is a major source of national pride. In 1970, China launched its first satellite, Dong Fang Hong I. In 2003, China became the third country to independently send humans into space, with Yang Liwei's spaceflight aboard Shenzhou 5. As of June 2013, ten Chinese nationals have journeyed into space. In 2011, China launched its first space station module, Tiangong-1, marking the first-step in a project to assemble a large manned station by 2020 (China, 2013).

Entrepreneurships in the US are left to individuals according to Laissez-faire doctrine. Funding usually comes from family members and friends, then later from angel investors, venture capitalists, and maybe from hedge funds for successful enterprises. In China, provincial and city government and officials play important roles in attracting talents, and helping entrepreneurs in funding, getting free land, housing buildings, and factories, and recruiting workers.

In recent years, many Chinese provincial and city governments have been organizing delegations traveling around the world to recruit talents. These government agencies provide candidates many perks to start businesses, especially high-tech businesses in their provinces or cities. The delegations organize free dinner events inviting overseas Chinese students, scientists, and scholars to five star hotels with gifts, and sometimes raffles for iPads. I attended a few of these dinner events. Wuxi City of Jiangsu Province organized one of the events. During the event Wuxi's Mayor Mr. Zhu Ke Jiang told us a story how he helped Zhengrong Shi, Ph.D., build SunTech Power. SunTech grew from one-person shop in 2000 to the world's largest producers of solar panels in five years. Dr. Shi became the richest person in China in 2006.

After receiving his master's degree from Shanghai Institute of Optics and Fine Mechanics in China, Zhengrong Shi received his Ph.D. from Australia's University of New South Wales. He became an Australian citizen, and worked at University of New South Wales. Dr. Shi heard from his friends that Wuxi City was recruiting entrepreneurs, especially from overseas. Dr. Shi met with Zhu Ke Jiang, then the Director of Office of Science and Technology of Jiangsu Province. Dr. Shi told Mr. Zhu that his only assets are the technologies he developed on solar energy and devices on his laptop computer and about $100,000 home equity in Australia. Mr. Zhu offered Dr. Shi 1 million RMB in capital from Wuxi city government, free housing, and free office space to form a joint venture SunTech Power in 2000. The city government received 50% of the shares of SunTech, and Dr. Shi received 50 percent for his technology intellectual property. The current incentives for oversea technical experts from Wuxi city are 1,000 square feet free housing for 3 years, and 1,000 square feet free office space for three years. The city provides capital, and also private venture funding. Venture funds are new phenomena in the last ten years in China.

Mr. Zhu has been promoted to the Mayor. During the event I attended, Mr. Zhu said that "I will give you my cell phone number, and you can call me twenty four hours a day, any day." At the end of the event, his cell phone number and all his staff attending the event were posted through the projection on the screen. China now is the largest producers and exporter of solar panels in the world. Mr. Zhu is an example that how China spot leadership talents and develops them, and how government fosters science and technology, and entrepreneurships.

The followings are China's 12th Five-Year Plan period (2011-2015) involves 7 strategic emerging industries (China's 12th Five-Year Plan period (2011-2015) involves 7 strategic emerging industries, 2012), namely:
1. New energy auto industry
2. Energy-saving and environmental protection industry
Energy-efficient industry
Advanced environmental protection industry
Resource recycling industry
3. New generation information technology industry
Next generation information network industry
Fundamental industry of core electronics
High-end software and new information service industry
4. Biology industry
Bio-pharmaceutical industry
Bio-medical engineering industry
Bio-breeding industry
Bio-manufacturing industry
5. High-end equipment manufacturing industry
Aviation equipment industry
Satellite and its application industry
Rail transportation equipment industry
Marine engineering equipment industry
Intelligent equipment-manufacturing industry
6. New energy industry

Nuclear energy technology industry
Wind energy industry
Solar energy industry
Biomass industry
7. New material industry
New functional material industry
Advanced structural material industry
High-performance composite material industry

Major projects

As provided by the Plan, the key development direction and main tasks for the 12th Five-Year Plan period also involve 20 key projects, including the following:

Key energy-saving technology and equipment industrialization project
Pilot project for equipment relating to key environmental protection technology and product industrialization
Important resource recycling project
Broadband China project
High-performance integrated circuits project
New-type flat panel display project
Internet of things (IOT) and cloud computing technology project
"Beneficial Information for the People" project
Protein-based biomedical products and vaccine project
High-performance medical treatment equipment project
Bio-breeding project
Bio-based material project
Aviation equipment project
Spatial infrastructure construction project
Advanced rail transport equipment and its key assemblies project
Marine engineering equipment project
Intelligent equipment-manufacturing project
New energy integrated application project
Key material upgradation project
New energy auto project

"None of the global warming discussions mention the word "nanotechnology." Yet nanotechnology will eliminate the need for fossil fuels within 20 years. If we captured 1% of 1% of the sunlight (1 part in 10,000) we could meet 100% of our energy needs without ANY fossil fuels. We can't do that today because the solar panels are too heavy, expensive, and inefficient. But there are new Nano engineered designs that are much more effective. Within five to six years, this technology will make a significant contribution. Within 20 years, it can provide all of our energy needs. The discussions talk about current trends continuing for the next century as if nothing is going to change. I think global warming is real but it has been modest thus far - 1 degree f. in 100 years. It would be concern if that continued or accelerated for a long period of time, but that's not going to happen. And it's not just environmental concern that will drive this; the $2 trillion we spend on energy is providing plenty of economic incentive. I don't see any disasters occurring in the next 10 years from this. However, I AM concerned about other environment issues. There are other reasons to want to move quickly away from fossil fuels including environmental pollution at every step and the geopolitical instability it causes." -- Ray Kurzweil

Chapter 15 Knowledge / Innovation Economy, Talents, Education and Teacher Pays

"Recruiting top students into teaching should be a national objective." -- Joel Klein, Chancellor of schools, New York City

"One unsatisfactory point is that we have not invested enough for the future, particularly in terms of developing human capital." -- Lee Kun-hee, Chairman of Samsung Electronics

Our world economy transitioned from an agricultural economy (the pre-industrial age) to industrial economy (the industrial age). Post-industrial / mass production economy (mid-1900s) transitioned to knowledge economy (late 1900s – 2000s) (Knowledge economy, 2013).

According to the five year plan of Singapore Agency for Science, Technology and Research (A*STAR)'s Science, Technology & Enterprise Plan 2015, Singapore's economy went through five stages: 1960 - 1969 labor intensive; 1970 – 1979 skill intensive; 1980 – 1989 capital intensive; 1990 – 1999 technology intensive; and 2000 – present, knowledge / innovation economy (A*STAR's Science, Technology & Enterprise Plan 2015, 2011).

In the Global Competitiveness Report 2013 – 2014, World Economic Forum measures Global Competitiveness Index (GCI) using 12 pillars: (1) institutions, (2) infrastructure, (3) macroeconomic environment, (4) health and primary education, (5) higher education and training, (6) good market efficiency, (7) labor market efficiency, (8) financial market development, (9) technology readiness, (10) market size, (11) business sophistication, and (12) innovation (Schwab, 2013).

Education is important for individuals and countries to successfully compete in the knowledge economy. The U.S. public education system is ranked 17th in the world according to a global report by education firm Pearson. The top five countries are

Finland, South Korea, Hong Kong, Japan and Singapore (Best Education In The World: Finland, South Korea Top Country Rankings, U.S. Rated Average, 2012). McKinsey & Company published a report "Closing the talent gap: Attracting and retaining top-third graduates to careers in teaching – An international and market research-based perspective". World's top performing education systems, Finland, South Korea, and Singapore, recruit 100 percent of teachers from top third of graduates. In the U.S., 23 percent teachers come from top third graduates, and only 14 percent teachers come from top third in high poverty schools (Aguster, Kihn, & Miller, 2010).

The quality of an education system cannot be better than the quality of the teachers in the system. Although the salary of teachers in the U.S. is high, but primary school teachers' salary as a percentage of GDP per capita is about 20 percent lower than that in Singapore and 60 percent lower than that in South Korea. U.S. primary school teacher's salary after 15 years is about 100 percent lower in that in Singapore and South Korea on a GDP per capita basis. In all three countries – South Korea, Finland, and Singapore, teaching is considered as a prestigious profession. Teacher selection and education are all centrally controlled in these three countries (Aguster, Kihn, & Miller, 2010).

U.S. has no centrally controlled teacher education and selection system. The U.S. federal government should setup a centrally controlled teacher selection and education system with funding to raise public school teachers' salaries. Private donations and organizations can also contribute the funding of the teacher salaries. Good education for children should not a privilege of the riches who can afford the best school districts or private schools. Good primary and secondary education should be available for all people. Talents selection and opportunities should be merit based, not family wealth based.

A country with large supplies of healthy high quality work force will compete successfully in the new knowledge economy. The country must have excellent macro environment such as affordable housing, good health care systems, sound primary and higher education system with a focus on STEM, and suitable foreign investment environments.

Seventy percent of Singapore population is ethnic Chinese. However Lee Kuan Yew, a Chinese descendent, chose English as the country's official language. Lee once recommended to a Chinese leader to change China's official language to English, but his suggestion went nowhere. If China had chosen English as its official language 35 years ago, its economy would have been more advanced than it is. China would be easier to attract international talents, and to learn Western's ways of thinking if English were its official language. Singapore grew from a very poor country with no natural resources in 1965 to a top country with one of the highest GDP per capita in less than 50 years. Both 5 million people Singapore and 1.3 billion people China have achieved about 10 percent GDP growth per year for the past 35 years.

USA has a large talent pool from around the world, sufficient natural resources, great infrastructure and industrial bases, and English as the official language. USA should and can to do better than China, Singapore, or South Korea have accomplished, if we determine to reform some difficult, but workable, problematic areas.

"As we gradually learn to harness the optimal computing capacity of matter, our intelligence will spread through the universe at (or exceeding) the speed of light, eventually leading to a sublime, universe wide awakening." -- Ray Kurzweil

Glossary

Amygdalae (singular: amygdala) are almond-shaped groups of nuclei located deep and medially within the temporal lobes of the brain in complex vertebrates, including humans. Shown in research to perform a primary role in the processing of memory and emotional reactions, the amygdalae are considered part of the limbic system.

Asthma is a common chronic inflammatory disease of the airways characterized by variable and recurring symptoms, reversible airflow obstruction and bronchospasm. Common symptoms include wheezing, coughing, chest tightness, and shortness of breath. Asthma is thought to be caused by a combination of genetic and environmental factors. Its diagnosis is usually based on the pattern of symptoms, response to therapy over time and spirometer.

Caloric restriction (CR), or calorie restriction, is a dietary regimen that is based on low calorie intake. "Low" can be defined relative to the subject's previous intake before intentionally restricting calories, or relative to an average person of similar body type. CR without malnutrition has been shown to work in a variety of species, among them yeast, fish, rodents and dogs to decelerate the biological aging process, resulting in longer maintenance of youthful health and an increase in both median and maximum lifespan.

Chaebol refers to a South Korean form of business conglomerate. They are typically global multinationals owning numerous international enterprises, controlled by a chairman who has power over all the operations. The term is often used in a context similar to that of the English word "conglomerate". The term was first used in 1984. There are several dozen large Korean family-controlled corporate groups which fall under this definition.

Central Provident Fund (CPF) is a compulsory comprehensive savings plan for working Singaporeans and permanent residents primarily to fund their retirement, health care, and housing needs. Central Provident Fund Board, a statutory board under the Ministry of Manpower, administers CPF. The employer has to contribute 16% of the employee's monthly gross salary while the employee contributes 20% of his monthly gross salary. The CPF was started on 1 July 1955.

A defined benefit pension plan is a type of pension plan in which an employer/sponsor promises a specified monthly benefit on retirement that is predetermined by a formula based on the employee's earnings history, tenure of service and age, rather than depending directly on individual investment returns. Traditionally, many governmental and public entities, as well as a large number of corporations, provided defined benefit plans, sometimes as a means of compensating workers in lieu of increased pay. A defined benefit plan is 'defined' in the sense that the benefit formula is defined and known in advance. Conversely, for a "defined contribution pension plan", the formula for computing the employer's and employee's contributions is defined and known in advance, but the benefit to be paid out is not known in advance. In the United States, 26 U.S.C. § 414(j) specifies a defined benefit plan to be any pension plan that is not a defined contribution plan where a defined contribution plan is any plan with individual accounts. A traditional pension plan that defines a benefit for an employee upon that employee's retirement is a defined benefit plan.

Detoxification (detox for short), is the physiological or medicinal removal of toxic substances from a living organism, including, but not limited to, the human body and additionally can refer to the period of withdrawal during which an organism returns to homeostasis after long-term use of an addictive substance. In medicine, detoxification can be achieved by decontamination of poison ingestion and the use of antidotes as well as techniques such as dialysis and (in a limited number of cases) chelation therapy.

Emotional intelligence (EI) is the ability to identify, assess, and control the emotions of oneself, of others, and of groups. It can be divided into ability EI and trait EI. The first published use of 'EQ' (Emotional Quotient) seems to be by Keith Beasley in 1987 in an article in the British Mensa magazine. However, the term became widely known with the publication of Goleman's Emotional Intelligence - Why it can matter more than IQ (1995). It is to this book's best-selling status that the term can attribute its popularity.

Eminent domain (United States, the Philippines), compulsory purchase (United Kingdom, New Zealand, and Ireland), resumption/compulsory acquisition (Australia), or expropriation (South Africa, Canada) is the power to take private property for public use by a state or national government. However, it can be legislatively delegated by the state to municipalities, government subdivisions, or even private persons or corporations when they are authorized to exercise functions of public character. The property may be taken either for government use or by delegation to third parties who will devote it to public or civic use or, in some cases, economic development. The most common uses of property taken by eminent domain are for government buildings and other facilities, public utilities, highways, and railroads; however, it may also be taken for reasons of public safety, as in the case of Centralia, Pennsylvania. Some jurisdictions require that the condemner offer to purchase the property before resorting to the use of eminent domain.

Eczema also known as atopic dermatitis is a form of chronic inflammation of the skin. Eczema is broadly applied to a range of persistent skin conditions. These include dryness and recurring skin rashes that are characterized by one or more of these symptoms: redness, skin edema (swelling), itching and dryness, crusting, flaking, blistering, cracking, oozing, or bleeding. Areas of temporary skin discoloration may appear and are sometimes due to healed injuries. Scratching open a healing lesion may result in scarring and may enlarge the rash.

Hedge fund is a pooled investment vehicle administered by a professional management firm, and often structured as a limited partnership, limited liability company, or similar vehicle. They are usually distinguished from private equity funds, which use the more illiquid investment strategies associated with private equity. Hedge funds invest in a diverse range of markets and use a wide variety of investment styles and financial instruments. The name "hedge fund" refers to the hedging techniques traditionally used by hedge funds, but hedge funds today do not necessarily hedge. Hedge funds are made available only to certain sophisticated or accredited investors and cannot be offered or sold to the general public. As such, they generally avoid direct regulatory oversight, bypass licensing requirements applicable to investment companies, and operate with greater flexibility than mutual funds and other investment funds.

High tech refers to technology that is at the cutting edge: the most advanced technology available. It is often used in reference to micro-electronics, rather than other technologies. The technology sector approach classifies industries according their technology intensity, product approach according to finished products: aerospace, automotive, artificial intelligence, biotechnology, semiconductors, information technology, electrical engineering, information systems, photonics, nanotechnology, nuclear physics, robotics, and telecommunications.

Limbic system (or paleomammalian brain) is a complex set of brain structures that lies on both sides of the thalamus, right under the cerebrum. It is not a separate system, but a collection of structures from the telencephalon, diencephalon, and mesencephalon. It includes the olfactory bulbs, hippocampus, amygdala, anterior thalamic nuclei, fornix, mamillary body, septum pellucidum, habenular commisure, cingulate gyrus, parahippocampal gyrus, limbic cortex, and limbic midbrain areas. The limbic system supports a variety of functions, including emotion, behavior, motivation, long-term memory, and olfaction. It appears to be primarily responsible for emotional life, and it has a great deal to do with the formation of memories.

Knowledge Economy is the use of knowledge to generate tangible and intangible values. Technology, and in particular knowledge technology (Artificial Intelligence), helps to transform a part of human knowledge to machines. This knowledge can be used by decision support systems in various fields and generate economic values.

Laissez-faire (or sometimes laisser-faire) is an economic environment in which transactions between private parties are free from government restrictions, tariffs, and subsidies, with only enough regulations to protect property rights. The phrase laissez-faire is French, and literally means, "let [them] do", but it broadly implies "let it be," "let them do as they will," or "leave it alone". Scholars generally believe a laissez-faire state or a completely free market has never existed and "doubtless never can exist".

Options contract in finance is a contract that gives the buyer (the owner) the rights, but not the obligation, to buy or sell underlying asset or instrument at specified strike prices on, or before a specified date. The seller incurs corresponding obligation to fulfill the transaction – that is to sell or buy – if the owner elects to "exercise" the options prior to expiration. The buyer pays a premium to the seller for this right. An option that conveys to the owner the right to buy something at a specific price is referred to as a call; an option that conveys the right of the owner to sell something at a specific price is referred to as a put. Both are commonly traded, but for clarity, the call option is more frequently discussed. Options are part of a larger class of financial instruments known as derivative products, or simply, derivatives.

Organic foods are foods that are produced using methods of organic farming – with limited modern synthetic inputs such as synthetic pesticides and chemical fertilizers, though organic pesticides, such as Bt toxin, are still used. Organic foods are also not processed using irradiation, industrial solvents, or chemical food additives. Organic food production is a heavily regulated industry, distinct from private gardening. Currently, the European Union, the United States, Canada, Japan and many other countries require producers to obtain special certification in order to market food as organic within their borders. In the context of these regulations, organic food is food produced in a way that complies with organic standards set by national governments and international organizations.

Payroll taxes are taxes that employers are required to pay when they pay their staff their salaries. Payroll taxes generally fall into two categories: deductions from an employee's wages and taxes paid by the employer based on the employee's wages. The first kind are taxes that employers are required to withhold from employees' wages, also known as withholding tax, pay-as-you-earn tax (PAYE), or pay-as-you-go tax (PAYG) and often to cover advance payment of income tax, social security contributions, and various insurances (e.g., unemployment and disability). The second kind is a tax that is paid from the employer's own funds and that is directly related to employing a worker. These can consist of fixed charges or be proportionally linked to an employee's pay. The charges paid by the employer usually cover the employer's funding of the social security system, and other insurance programs.

Price-to-earnings ratio, or P–E ratio, or P/E ratio, is an equity valuation multiple. It is defined as market price per share divided by annual earnings per share. "Trailing P–E" uses net income for the most recent 12-month period, divided by the weighted average number of common shares in issue during the period. This is the most common meaning of "P–E" if no other qualifier is specified. Monthly earnings data for individual companies are not available, and in any case usually fluctuate seasonally, so the previous four quarterly earnings reports are used and earnings per share are updated quarterly.

Quantitative easing (QE) is an unconventional monetary policy used by central banks to prevent the money supply falling when standard monetary policy has become ineffective. A central bank implements quantitative easing by buying specified amounts of financial assets from commercial banks and other private institutions thus increases the monetary base. This is distinguished from the more usual policy of buying or selling government bonds in order to keep market interest rates at a specified target value.

Regenerative medicine is the process of replacing or regenerating human cells, tissues or organs, to restore or establish normal function. This field holds the promise of regenerating damaged tissues and organs in the body by replacing damaged tissue and/or by stimulating the body's own repair mechanisms to heal previously irreparable tissues or organs. Regenerative medicine also includes the possibility of growing tissues and organs in the laboratory and safely implants them when the body cannot heal itself. This can potentially solves the problem of the shortage of organs available for donation, and the problem of organ transplant rejection if the organ's cells are derived from the patient's own tissue or cells.

Return on capital (ROC) is a ratio used in finance, valuation, and accounting. The ratio is estimated by dividing the after-tax operating income (NOPAT) by the book value of invested capital.

ROC = (Net Operating Profit - Adjusted Taxes) / (Book Value of Debt + Book Value of Equity – Cash)

Sovereign wealth fund (SWF) is a state-owned investment fund investing in real and financial assets such as stocks, bonds, real estate, precious metals, or in alternative investments such as private equity fund or hedge funds. Sovereign wealth funds invest globally. Most SWFs are funded by revenues from commodity exports or from foreign-exchange reserves held by the central bank.

Stem cells are undifferentiated biological cells. Stem cells can differentiate into specialized cells and can divide (through mitosis) to produce more stem cells. They are found in multicellular organisms. In mammals, there are two broad types of stem cells: embryonic stem cells, which are isolated from the inner cell mass of blastocysts, and adult stem cells, which are found in various tissues. In adult organisms, stem cells and progenitor cells act as a repair system for the body, replenishing adult tissues. In a developing embryo, stem cells can differentiate into all the specialized cells - ectoderm, endoderm and mesoderm - but also maintain the normal turnover of regenerative organs, such as blood, skin, or intestinal tissues. There are three accessible sources of autologous adult stem cells in humans: Bone marrow, Adipose tissue (lipid cells), and Blood.

STEM fields or STEM education is an acronym for the fields of study in the categories of science, technology, engineering, and mathematics. The term is typically used in addressing education policy and curriculum choices in schools from kindergarten through college to improve the nation's competitiveness in technology development. It has implications for workforce development, national security concerns and immigration policy.

Whole foods are foods that are unprocessed and unrefined, or processed and refined as little as possible, before being consumed. Whole foods typically do not contain added salt, carbohydrates, or fat. Examples of whole foods include unpolished grains, beans, fruits, vegetables and non-homogenized dairy products. Although originally all human food was whole food, one of the earliest uses of the term post-industrial age was in 1960 when the leading organic food organization called the Soil Association opened a shop in the name selling organic and whole grain products in London, UK. The term is often confused with organic food, but whole foods are not necessarily organic, nor are organic foods necessarily whole.

Bibliography

Contitution of the People's Republic of China. (1982, December 4). Retrieved 2013, from People's Daily Online: http://english.people.com.cn

Fortune Global 500. (1996). Retrieved 2013, from Fortune China: http://www.fortunechina.com

Chinese capitalism The long march backwards. (2008, October 2). Retrieved from The Economist: http://www.economist.com

*A*STAR's Science, Technology & Enterprise Plan 2015.* (2011). Retrieved from Singapore Agency for Science, Technology and Research: www.a-star.edu.sg

Go East, young bureaucrat - Emerging Asia can teach the West a lot about government. (2011, March 17). Retrieved from The Economist's : http://www.economist.com

Samsung and its attractions Asia's new model company. (2011, 10 1). Retrieved from The Economist: http://www.economist.com

The Founding Fathers Tried to Warn Us About the Threat From a Two-Pary System. (2011, July 7). Retrieved from Washintons Blog: www.washingtonsblog.com

Best Education In The World: Finland, South Korea Top Country Rankings, U.S. Rated Average. (2012, November). Retrieved from Huffington Post: http://www.huffingtonpost.com/2012/11/27/best-education-in-the-wor_n_2199795.html.

China's 12th Five-Year Plan period (2011-2015) involves 7 strategic emerging industries. (2012). Retrieved from China Briefing: http://www.china-briefing.com

Top ten chaebol now almost 80% of Korean economy. (2012, August 28). Retrieved from Hankyoreh: http://www.hani.co.kr

Why Singapore Has the Cleanest Government Money Can Buy. (2012, January 24). Retrieved from Bloomberg: http://www.bloomberg.coml

100 Best-Performing CEOs in the World. (2013, January). Retrieved November 8, 2013, from Harvard Business Review: http://www.hbr.org

About MTI. (2013). Retrieved from Ministry of Trade and Industry Singapore: http://www.mti.gov.sg

Atherosclerosis. (2013). Retrieved 2013, from Wikepedia: http://en.wikipedia.org

Bankruptcy of Lehman Brothers. (2013). Retrieved November 2013, from Wikipedia: http://en.wikipedia.org

Breakfast. (2013). Retrieved from Wikipedia: http://en.wikipedia.org

Calorie restriction. (2013). Retrieved 2013, from Wikipedia: http://en.wikipedia.org

Central Provident Fund - Ministry of Manpower. (2013). Retrieved 2013, from Ministry of Manpower: http://www.mom.gov.sg

Chemical energy. (2013). Retrieved 2013, from Wikipedia: http://en.wikipedia.org

China. (2013). Retrieved from Wikipedia: http://en.wikipedia.org

CIA The World Factbook. (2013). Retrieved from Central Intelligence Agency: https://www.cia.gov

Cortisone. (2013). Retrieved 2013, from Wikipedia: http://en.wikipedia.org

Detoxification. (2013). Retrieved November 2, 2013, from Wikipedia: http://en.wikipedia.org/wiki/Detoxification

Dinner. (2013). Retrieved 2013, from Wikipedia: http://en.wikipedia.org

Eminent domain. (2013). Retrieved from Wikipedia: http://en.wikipedia.org

Foreign exchange reserves of the People's Republic of China. (2013). Retrieved 2013, from Wikipedia: http://en.wikipedia.org

Fortune Global 500. (2013). Retrieved 2013, from Fortune: http://money.cnn.com

Government-owned corporation. (2013). Retrieved from Wikipedia: http://en.wikipedia.org

Guidance for Industry: A Food Labeling Guide (14. Appendix F: Calculate the Percent Daily Value for the Appropriate Nutrients). (2013). Retrieved 2013, from U.S. Food and Drug Administration: http://www.fda.gov

Housing & Development Board. (2013). Retrieved from HDB InfoWEB: http://www.hdb.gov.sg

human nutrition. (2013). Retrieved 2013, from Encyclopædia Britannica: http://www.britannica.com

IMF Report for Selected Countries and Subjects. (2013). Retrieved November 8, 2013, from International Monetary Fund: http://http://www.imf.org

Increase your Stem Cells Naturally! (2013). Retrieved 2013, from www.afa.com: http://www.afa.com

Knowledge economy. (2013). Retrieved November 8, 2013, from Wikipedia: http://http://en.wikipedia.org

List of countries by tax rates. (2013). Retrieved from Wikipedia: http://en.wikipedia.org

List of State-owned enterprises in China. (2013). Retrieved from Wikipedia: http://en.wikipedia.org

MSN Money Investing - Key Ratios. (2013). Retrieved from MSN Money: http://investing.money.msn.com

MyPlate. (2013). Retrieved 2013, from Wikipedia: http://en.wikipedia.org

Nourish - Fats. (2013). Retrieved 2013, from The Frankline Institute: http://www.fi.edu

Nutrient. (2013). Retrieved 2013, from Wikipedia: http://en.wikipedia.org

On Contradiction. (2013). Retrieved 2013, from Wikipedia: http://en.wikipedia.org

Organic food. (2013). Retrieved 2013, from Wikipedia: http://en.wikipedia.org

People's commune. (2013). Retrieved 2013, from Wikipedia: http://en.wikipedia.org

Press Releases. (2013). Retrieved 2013, from Questcor: http://ir.questcor.com

Protein nutrient. (2013). Retrieved 2013, from Wikipedia: http://en.wikipedia.org

Public housing in Singapore. (2013). Retrieved from Wikipedia: http://en.wikipedia.org

Return on Capital. (2013). Retrieved November 9, 2013, from Wikipedia: http://en.wikipedia.org

Samsung. (2013). Retrieved from Wikipedia: http://en.wikipedia.org

Shenzhen. (2013). Retrieved 2013, from Wikipedia: http://en.wikipedia.org

Smoking in China. (2013). Retrieved from Wikipedia: http://en.wikipedia.org

Social Security and Medicare tax rates; maximum taxable earnings. (2013). Retrieved from Social Security Administration: http://ssa-custhelp.ssa.gov

Solar energy. (2013). Retrieved 2013, from Wikipedia: http://en.wikipedia.org

Sovereign Wealth Fund Rankings. (2013). Retrieved 2013, from Sovereign Wealth Fund Institute: http://www.swfinstitute.org

Stem cell. (2013). Retrieved 2013, from Wikipedia: http://en.wikipedia.org

Stem cell laws and policy in the United States. (2013). Retrieved 2013, from Wikipedia: http://en.wikipedia.org

The Evolutionary Layers of the Human Brain. (2013). Retrieved 2013, from The Brain from Top to Bottom: http://thebrain.mcgill.ca

The Incredible Bionic Man. (2013). Retrieved 2013, from SmithsonianChannel.com: http://www.smithsonianchannel.com

Vilayanur S. Ramachandran. (2013). Retrieved from Wikipedia: http://en.wikipedia.org

Vitamin. (2013). Retrieved 2013, from Wikipedia: http://en.wikipedia.org

Vitamin C. (2013). Retrieved from Wikipedia: http://en.wikipedia.org

Whole food. (2013). Retrieved 2013, from Wikipedia: http://en.wikipedia.org

Aguster, B., Kihn, P., & Miller, M. (2010, September). *Closing the talent gap: Attracting and retaining top-third graduates to careers in teaching – An international and market research-based perspective.* Retrieved from McKinsey & Company: http://www.mckinseyonsociety.com/

An. (2011, December). *China publishes the second most scientific papers in international journals in 2010: report.* Retrieved from Xinhua: http://news.xinhuanet.com

Belvedere, M. (2013, November 1). *Obamacare lacks key cost control: Mayo Clinic CEO.* Retrieved from CNBC: http://www.cnbc.com

Bloomberg. (2013). *World Most Efficient Health Care.* Retrieved November 8, 2013, from Bloomberg: http://www.bloomberg.com

Boyd, R. (2008, March 31). *The last days of Bear Stearns*. Retrieved from CNN: http://money.cnn.com

Bradberry, T., & Greaves, J. (2009). *Emotional Intelligence 2.0.* TalentSmart.

Butterfield, F. (1976, September 10). *Mao Tse-Tung: Father of Chinese Revolution*. Retrieved 2013, from New York Times: http://www.nytimes.com

Callick, R. (2008, May 27). *The city-state of Singapore may have a fix for America's healthcare woes*. Retrieved from The American: http://www.american.com

Callis, R. R., & Kresin, M. (2013). *Residential Vacancies and Homeownership in the Third Quarter 2013*. Retrieved from U.S. Census Bureau: http://www.census.gov/housing/hvs/files/currenthvspress.pdf

Campbell, T. C., & Campbell II, T. M. (2006). *The China Study: The Most Comprehensive Study of Nutrition Ever Conducted And the Startling Implications for Diet, Weight Loss, And Long-term Health.* BenBella Books.

Canton, J. P. (2006). *The Extreme Future The Top Ten Trends That Will Reshape the World in the Next 20 years.* Penguin Books Ltd.

Chang, G. G. (2013, June 23). *China's Maoist Vision: A City Of 260 Million People*. Retrieved 2013, from Forbes: http://www.forbes.com

Chow, J. (2013, September 24). *China Goes Postal for Stamp Collecting*. Retrieved from The Wall Street Journal: http://online.wsj.com

Colvin, G. (2010). *Desperately seeking math and science majors*. Retrieved from CNN Money: http://money.cnn.com

Conover, C. J. (2011, October 25). *Is Medicare a Ponzi Scheme?* Retrieved from The American: http://www.american.com

de Grey, A., & Rae, M. (2008). *Ending Aging: The Rejuvenation Breakthroughs That Could Reverse Human Aging in Our Lifetime.* St. Martin's Griffin.

Dorsey, P. (2008). *The Little Book That Builds Wealth: The Knockout Formula for Finding Great Investments* . Wiley.

Ebeling, A. (2013, October 31). *The $500 Tweak To The Healthcare Flexible Spending Use It Or Lose It Rule.* Retrieved from Forbes: http://www.forbes.com

Fournier, R. (2013, January 14). *Talkin' About Revolution: 6 Reasons Why the Two-Party System May Become Obsolete - No Labels.* Retrieved from National Journal: http://www.nationaljournal.com/

Fuhrman MD, J. (1995). *Fasting and Eating for Health - A Medical Doctor's Program for Conquering Disease.* St. Martin's Griffin.

Goleman, D. (2005). *Emotional Intelligence: Why It Can Matter More Than IQ* . Bantam Books.

Goleman, D. (2007). *Social Intelligence: The New Science of Human Relationships.* Bantam.

Greenblatt, J. (2010). *The Little Book That Still Beats the Market.* Wiley.

Han, K. (2012, June 8). *The sorry state of unions in Singapore.* Retrieved 2013, from Waging Non Violence: http://wagingnonviolence.org

Holford, P. (2005). *The New Optimum Nutrition Bible Paperback.* Crossing Press.

Howard, P. K. (2012, August 3). *Reform Is Not Enough: The Federal Government Needs a Complete Makeover.* Retrieved from The Atlantic: http://www.theatlantic.com

Koenig, B. (2013, September). *Facebook's Zuckerberg gives himself a label.* Retrieved from CNN: http://politicalticker.blogs.cnn.com

Kurzweil, R. (2006). *The Singularity Is Near: When Humans Transcend Biology.* Penguin Books .

Maccaro, J. (2005). *90 Day Immune System Revised: This vital life-saving information will help you.* Siloam.

Manjoo, F. (2013). *Silicon Valley Has an Arrogance Problem. It's Too Proud, Too Self-Centered, and That's Not Good For Anyone.* Wall Street Journal.

Mao, T.-T. (1937, August). *On Contridiction.* Retrieved 2013, from Marxists: http://www.marxists.org

Matthews, M. (2012, August 21). Think Social Security's Trust Fund Is A Scam? Medicare Has One Too. Forbes.

McFarlane, K. (2013, May). *Is China's frenzy of city-building a fragile bubble?* . Retrieved from Jamaica observer: http://www.jamaicaobserver.com/columns

Morrison, W. M. (2013). *China's Economic Rise: History, Trends,* . Congressional Research Service.

Naik, G. (2013, March 22). *Science Fiction Comes Alive as Researchers Grow Organs in Lab.* Retrieved 2013, from Wall Street Journal: http://online.wsj.com

Nojima, Y., Hirose, T., Tachibana, K., Tanaka, T., Shi, L., Doshen, J., et al. (1993). The 4F9 Antigen Is a Member of the Tetra Spans Transmembrane Protein Family and Functions as an Accessory Molecule in T Cell Activation and Adhesion. *Cellular Immunology*, 152.

NOVA, s. (2005). Mirror Neurons.

Orloski, A. (2002, June 30). *DuPont celebrates 200 years; reorganizes businesses.* Retrieved from Packaging World: http://www.packworld.com

Pauling, L., & Rath, M. (1990). Hypothesis: Lipoprotein(a) is a surrogate for ascorbate. *Proceedings of the National Academy of Sciences (PNAS)*.

Pfuntner, A., Wier, M., Lauren, M., & Steiner, M. C. (2013, January). *Costs for Hospital Stays in the United States, 2010*. Retrieved 2013, from Agency for Healthcare Research and Quality: http://www.hcup-us.ahrq.gov

Pollack, A. (2012, December 29). Questcor Finds Profits, at $28,000 a Vial. New York Times.

Porter, M. E. (1998). *"Clusters and the New Economics of Competition".Harvard Business Review. December: 77–90*.

Rinzler, C. A. (2011). *Nutrition For Dummies*. For Dummies.

Russ, A. C. (2010, November 4). *What is a Security?* Retrieved from North Carolina Bar Association: http://businesslaw.ncbar.org

Salsman, R. M. (2011, September 27). *Social Security is Much Worse Than a Ponzi Scheme - and Here's How to End It*. Retrieved from Forbes: http://www.forbes.com

Schreyogg, J., & Lim, M. K. (2004, March). Health-Care Reform in Singapore - Twenty Years of Medical Savings Accounts. *CESifo DICE Report*.

Schwab, K. (2013). *The Global Competitiveness Report 2013 – 2014*. Retrieved from World Economic Forum: www.weforum.org

Sherk, J. (2008). *UAW Workers Actually Cost the Big Three Automakers $70 an Hour*. Retrieved from The Heritage Foundation published an article:: http://www.heritage.org

Shytle, D., Tan, J., Ehrhart, J., Smith, A., Sanberg, C., Sanberg, P., et al. (2010). Effects of blue-green algae extracts on the proliferation of human adult stem cells in vitro: a preliminary study. *Medical Science Monitor*.

Siddiqui, K. (2010). The Political Economy of Development in SingaporeThe Political Economy of Development in Singapore. *Research in Applied Economics*.

SSA. (2013). *A SUMMARY OF THE 2013 ANNUAL REPORTS Social Security and Medicare Boards of Trustees*. Retrieved November 8, 2013, from Social Security Administration: http://http://www.ssa.gov

Stern, D. (2004). *The Present Moment in Psychotherapy and Everyday Life (New York: Norton, 2004), 76.* . W. W. Norton & Company.

Stump, S. (2013, October 1). *Man drives record 3 million miles in the same 1966 Volvo*. Retrieved 2013, from Today News: http://www.today.com

Teitelbaum, R. (2013, September 20). Berkshire Billionaire Found With More Shares Than Gates.

Walford, R., & Weindruch, R. (1988). *The Retardation of Aging and Disease by Dietary Restriction.* , T, 1988, .

Wayne, J. (2013). *What Percentage of Payroll Vs. Income for a Small Business?* Retrieved 2013, from Chron: http://smallbusiness.chron.com

Yew, L. K. (1998). *The Singapore Story: Memoirs of Lee Kuan Yew*. Prentice Hall College Div.

Yoon, S. (2012 , November 21). *Reining In South Korea's Chaebol*. Retrieved from Bloomberg Business Week: http://www.businessweek.com

Yuen, B. (2007). Squatter No More: Singapore Social Housing. *Global Urban Development*.

Acknowledgment

I wish to personally thank the following people for their contributions to my inspiration and knowledge and other help in life and in creating this book:

I wish to thank for my parents' love and support throughout my life. My sister Heying for taking care my daughter Marilyn when she was in China for 3 years. My two uncles, James Wen and George Wen, helped me to come to the USA to pursuing graduate studies. I would also like to thank for my wife Jia. Without your love and support, this book would not be possible.

I also wish to thank a few great teachers throughout my life: my high school English teacher Ms. Yu. You taught English in a simple and easy way. I never thought that one day I would write a book, and in English. Dr. Bonnie Sampsell of State University of New York encouraged me to pursue of my interests. I'd like to thank you Dr. Robert Mocker of St. John's University for pushing me forwards and providing the chance meeting Warren Buffett.

Thank you to the following individuals who without their contributions and support this book would not have been written: Eugene Walton for your periodical checking and pushing on my progresses. Zach Kau for your encouragements.

About the Author

Linkun Shi, CPA, was born in Kunming City, Yunnan Province in southwestern China at the beginning of China's Cultural Revolution. Linkun graduated from Kunming Number One High School. He received his Bachelor of Science from Sun Yat-sen (Zhongshan) University, China. He received his Master Degree in biology from State University of New York. He is an author of a scientific research paper on molecular immunology when he was working at Dana-Farber Cancer Institute, Harvard Medical School. He also worked at Pfizer and Merck. Subsequently he obtained a MBA from St. John's University also on full scholarships. He worked for a couple accounting firms as an audit associate with various industries, lastly with a focus on hedge funds and financial service firms. He received his New York CPA license in 2000. He is a Health Care Financial Analyst at the U.S. Department of Housing and Urban Development. Prior to that, he was a Project Manager at New York Multifamily Hub of the same federal agency. He is a registered investment adviser. He, his wife Jia and three children live in New York City. You can reach him at linkunshi@gmail.com.

Index

A

A*STAR, **161**
A.G. Lafley, 45
Aging, 105
Alan Mulally, 43
Allergies, **100**
amygdala, **33**
Aphaizonmenonflos-aquae, **106**
Asthma, 100
atherosclerosis, **95**
ATP, **88**

B

Benjamin Graham, **29**
Blake Nordstrom, 44

C

calorie, **14**, **90**, **96**, **164**
calorie restriction, **13**
carbohydrates, **86**
Carbohydrates, 92
Cardiovascular Diseases, 95
Carlos Brito, 42
Carol Meyrowitz, 45
Central Provident Fund, **126**
chaebol, **138**
Charlie Ergen, 44
Charlie Munger, **29**
cheap companies, **38**
Christopher Connor, 45

contradiction, **117**
Contrarian Investors, 31
Cortisone, **103**
Cultural Revolution, 7

D

Daniel Abounmrad, 44
Daniel Goleman, **32**
David Cote, 44
David Novak, 42
David Pyott, 44
David Simon, 42
Deng Xiaoping, 7
Dieting, 84
DNA, **87**

E

Eczema, 100
Ed Clark, 43
education, **162**
Education, 161
Elon Musk, **22**, 40
emotional, **14**
Emotional Intelligence, 31
Emotional Intelligence Quotient, **11**
Energy, 90
Entrepreneurships, 155, **156**
EQ, **11**

F

Fair Prices, 29

fats, 87
Fats, 93
Formula, 37
Fortune 500, **134**
Frank Riboud, 44
Fred Goodwin, 45
Fred Smith, 42
Fujio Mitarai, 43

G

George Paz, 44
glycogen, **87**
Gordon Nixon, 45
Graham Mckay, 45
Great Leap Forward, **112**
great people, **37**

H

Harvard Medical School, **8**
Health Care, 144, 147
High-Techs, 155
Home Ownerships, 144
Howard Schultz, 41
Hugh Grant, 42
Hugh Hayek, 45

I

immune system, **100**
Innovation Economy, 161

J

Jamie Dimon, 39
Jeffrey Bezos, 40
Jeffrey Boyd, 45
Jeffrey Immelt, 41
Jim Sinegal, 40

Jim Skinner, 43
Joe Tucci, 43
John Martin, 44
Joint Pains, 100, **104**
Jose Carbajal, 42
Jose Gobrielli, 44
Joseph Papa, 44

K

Kenneth Chenault, 44
Kenning Kagermann, 45

L

Laissez-faire, **156**
Lakshmi Mittal, 41
Larry Ellison, 43
Larry Fink, 42
Lars Rebien S., 42
Lawrence Page, 39
Lee Kuan Yew, **123**
Lee Kun-hee, 41
Leslie Moonres, 44
Lew Frankfort, 41
limbic system, **33**
Limbic system, **33**
Linus Pauling, **95**
Lipids, 93
lipoprotein A, **96**
Long Term Prospective, 82

M

Mao Thought, **109**
Marc Benioff, 45
Marissa A. Mayer, 41
Marius Kloppers, 43
Mark Donegan, 45

Mark Hurd, 43
Mark Papa, 41
Mark Zuckerberg, 39
Medical Savings Accounts, **148**

metabolism, **86**
Michael Kors, 41
Michael O'Leary, 45
Micronutrients, 94
Miles White, 42
Minerals, 94
Ministry of Trade and Industry, **155**
Mirror neurons, **34**
Mirror Neurons, 31, **35**
Mitochondria, **106**
Morris Chang, 45

P

P/E ratios, **30**
Paolo Rocca, 45
Patience, 82
Patrick Daniel, 44
Paul Otellini, 44
People's Communes, **112**
Peter Loscher, 44
Peter Rose, 44
proteins, **87**
Proteins, 93

Q

Questcor Pharmaceuticals, **103**

R

Return on Capital, 26
Revenue per Employee, 28

Rex Tillerson, 43
Robert Lane, 44
Robert Mockler, **9**
Robin Yanhong Li, 41
ROC, 26

S

Sam Palmisano, 43
Samsung Electronics, **138**
Scurvy, **94**
Sergrey Brin, 39
Shengzhen, **9**
Shenzhen, **119**
skipping diner, **91**
Sleeping Disorders, 100, **103**
Sovereign Funds, **137**
state owned enterprises, **128**
STEM, 155
Stem cells, **106**
Steve Wynn, 41
Stewart Horejsi, **21**
Sun Tzu, **31**
Sun Yat-sen University, **8**
SunTech Power, **157**

T

Tadashi Yanai, 41
Talents, 161
Teacher Pays, 161
Terry Leahy, 42
Timothy Cook, 41
toxins, **87**
Travis Bradberry, **34**

Treasury Inflation-Protected Securities, 25

Triple Flex, **104**

U

Unions, 142

V

Vilayanur S. Ramachandran, **34**

Vitamins, 94, 96

W

Wang Chuan-fu, 44
Warren Buffett, **9**, 40
Warren East, 43
William Doyle, 45
wonderful company, **24**

Y

Yun Jong-yong, 41

Z

Zhongshan University, **8**

www.ingramcontent.com/pod-product-compliance
Lightning Source LLC
Chambersburg PA
CBHW051651170526
45167CB00001B/417